CW01371899

lonely planet KIDS

A KID'S GUIDE TO
PARIS

LET THE ADVENTURE BEGIN!

by Paige Towler

Project Editor: Priyanka Lamichhane
Designers: Carolyn Sewell, Andrew Mansfield
Publishing Director: Piers Pickard
Publisher: Rebecca Hunt
Art Director: Emily Dubin
Print Production: Nigel Longuet

The Lonely Planet Kids Travel Guides series is produced in partnership with the WonderLab Group, LLC.

Special thanks to our city consultant, Nicola Williams, and editor, Rose Davidson.

Published in May 2025 by Lonely Planet Global Limited
CRN: 554153
ISBN: 9781837585274
www.lonelyplanet.com/kids
© Lonely Planet 2025
10 9 8 7 6 5 4 3 2 1
Printed in Malaysia

All rights reserved. No part of this publication may be reproduced, stored in a retrieval system or transmitted in any form by any means, electronic, mechanical, photocopying, recording or otherwise except brief extracts for the purpose of review, without the written permission of the publisher. Lonely Planet and the Lonely Planet logo are trademarks of Lonely Planet and are registered in the US Patent and Trademark Office and in other countries.

Although the author and Lonely Planet have taken all reasonable care in preparing this book, we make no warranty about the accuracy or completeness of its content and, to the maximum extent permitted, disclaim all liability from its use.

STAY IN TOUCH
lonelyplanet.com/contact

Lonely Planet Office:
IRELAND
Digital Depot, Roe Lane (off Thomas St),
Digital Hub, Dublin 8, D08 TCV4, Ireland

MIX
Paper | Supporting responsible forestry
FSC™ C021741

Paper in this book is certified against the Forest Stewardship Council™ standards. FSC™ promotes environmentally responsible, socially beneficial and economically viable management of the world's forests.

lonely planet KIDS

A KID'S GUIDE TO
PARIS

LET THE ADVENTURE BEGIN!

by Paige Towler

CONTENTS

- How to Use This Book — 10
- Welcome to Paris! — 12
- Mapping It Out — 14
- Getting Around Town — 18
- Places to Play — 32
- What a View! — 44
- Let's Eat! — 56
- Stroll the Champs-Élysées — 70
- A Monumental City — 82
- The Wild Side — 94
- Going Green — 106
- Secrets of the City — 118
- What's the Difference? — 130
- Index — 134
- Resources — 138
- Credits — 139

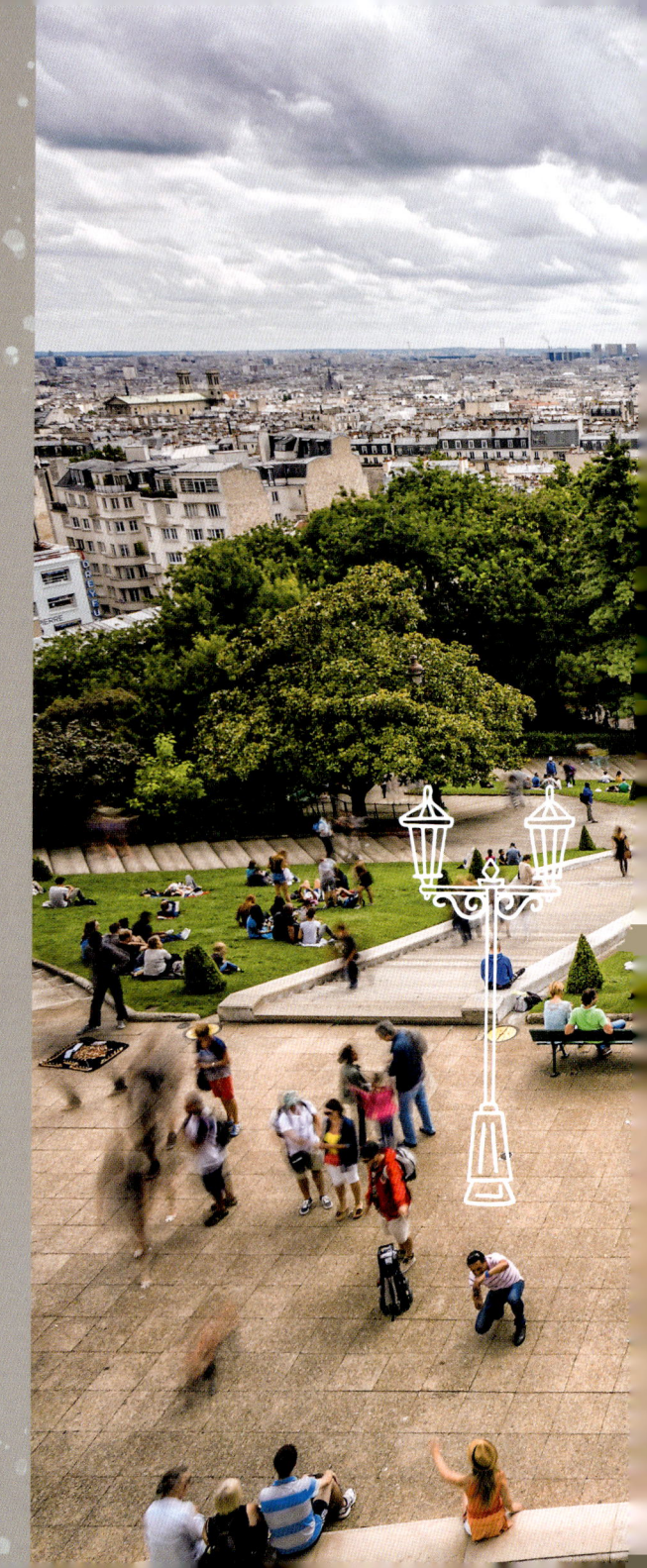

IMAGE: Square Louise Michel, Montmartre.

8 A Kid's Guide to PARIS

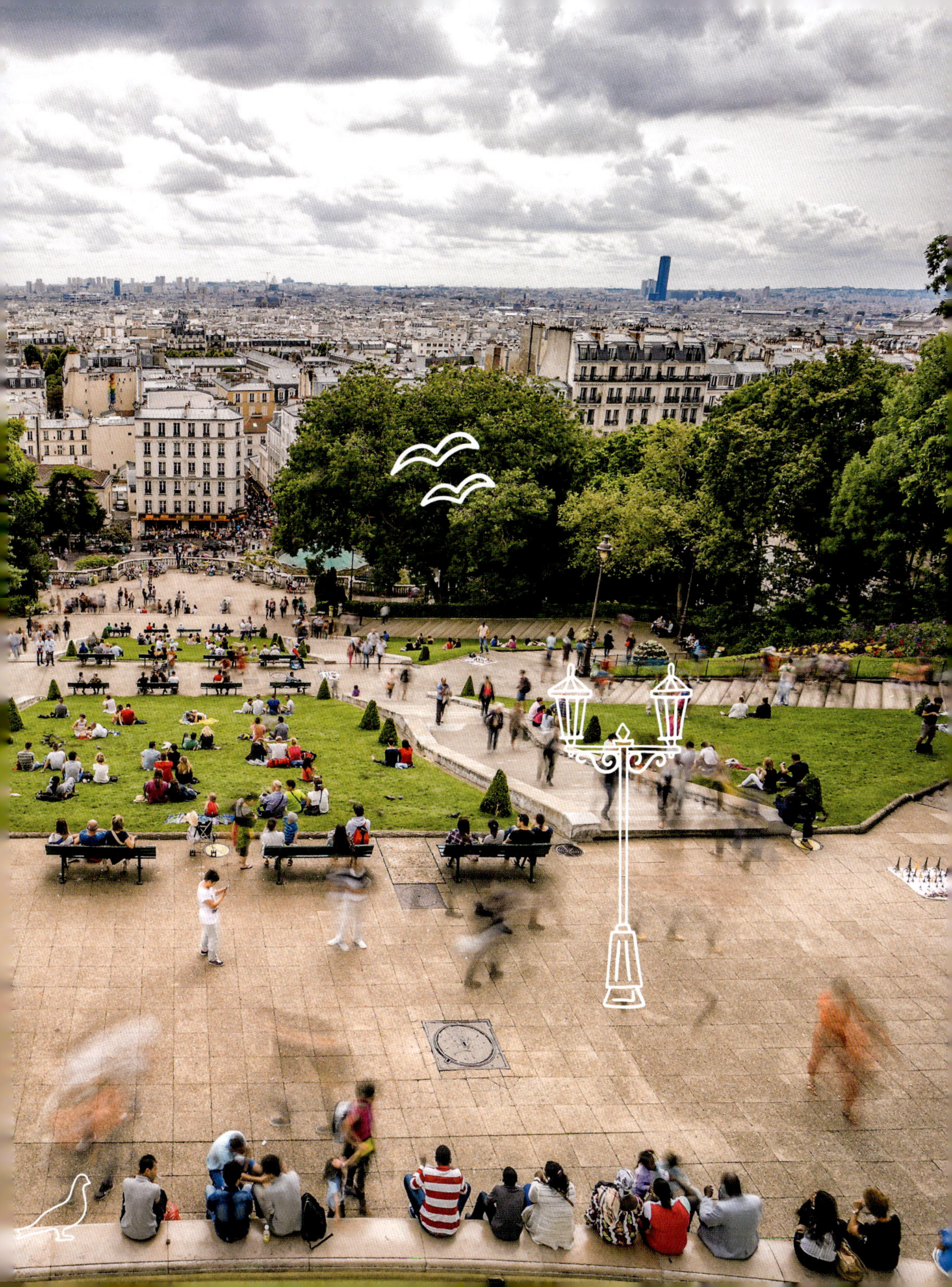

HOW TO USE THIS BOOK

Are you in search of a city's most delish desserts or wild about urban wilderness? Maybe you want to check out some places to play or discover the history and mysteries of the city. Or, perhaps, all of the above? Each chapter of this book has a unique theme. You can read the book from beginning to end or dip in and out! Don't forget to scour each page for fun facts, places, people and more. Here are some highlighted features in the book.

Like collecting facts and stats?

Check these out.

Here are a few translations for phrases you will find in this book.

ENGLISH / FRENCH

Hello / Bonjour
Goodbye / Au revoir
Thank you! / Merci!
Let's go! / Allons-y!
That's fun! / Ça, c'est cool!

10 A Kid's Guide to PARIS

What makes this city tick?

Stroll along the Champs-Élysées on pages 70–81 or explore the city's many monuments on pages 82–93.

Curious about the weirdest, wackiest and most unheard-of spots?

'Secrets of the City' is on pages 118-129.

Need something to do while travelling by train, bus, plane or car?

Look for 'What's the Difference?' on pages 130-133.

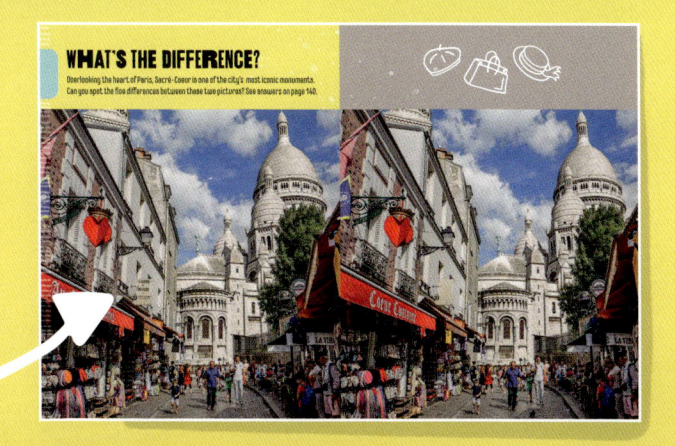

PARIS 11

WELCOME TO PARIS!

Bienvenue – welcome! Paris is the City of Light. Here, you can go up the iconic Eiffel Tower for stunning views. Come face-to-face with the magical *Mona Lisa* at the Louvre. Visit Notre-Dame Cathedral to see gargoyles high in the towers.

Up for an adventure? Take a boat on the Seine River. For spooky fun, explore the underground catacombs if you dare!

These are just some of the iconic sights in Paris – but the city is also full of hidden and unexpected places. Explore a real sewer, or check out a museum dedicated to old carnival rides that you can actually ride! Inside this guide, you'll find all this and so much more. Bon voyage!

IMAGES: View of the Eiffel Tower from Pont Alexandre III (right); Pont Alexandre III (opposite).

CITY OF LIGHT

You may have heard that Paris is the City of Light – but what does that mean? As early as the 1660s, Paris lined its streets with candlelit lamps. Today, the city is even more bejewelled at night, with sparkling electric streetlamps, building signs and more. Even the Eiffel Tower lights up at night – and sometimes in different colours for special events!

At the turn of each hour from dusk to 1 a.m., lights on the Eiffel Tower twinkle for five minutes.

BONJOUR

MAPPING IT OUT

FRANCE

- HAUTS-DE-FRANCE
- NORMANDY
- PARIS
- GRAND EST
- BRITTANY
- PAYS DE LA LOIRE
- CENTRE-VAL DE LOIRE
- BOURGOGNE-FRANCHE-COMTÉ
- NOUVELLE-AQUITAINE
- AUVERGNE-RHÔNE-ALPES
- OCCITANIE
- PROVENCE-ALPES-CÔTE D'AZUR
- CORSICA

As well as having 20 different arrondissements (neighbourhoods), Paris is divided into two sections by the Seine River. These areas are Rive Gauche (the Left Bank) and Rive Droite (the Right Bank).

SEINE

A Kid's Guide to PARIS

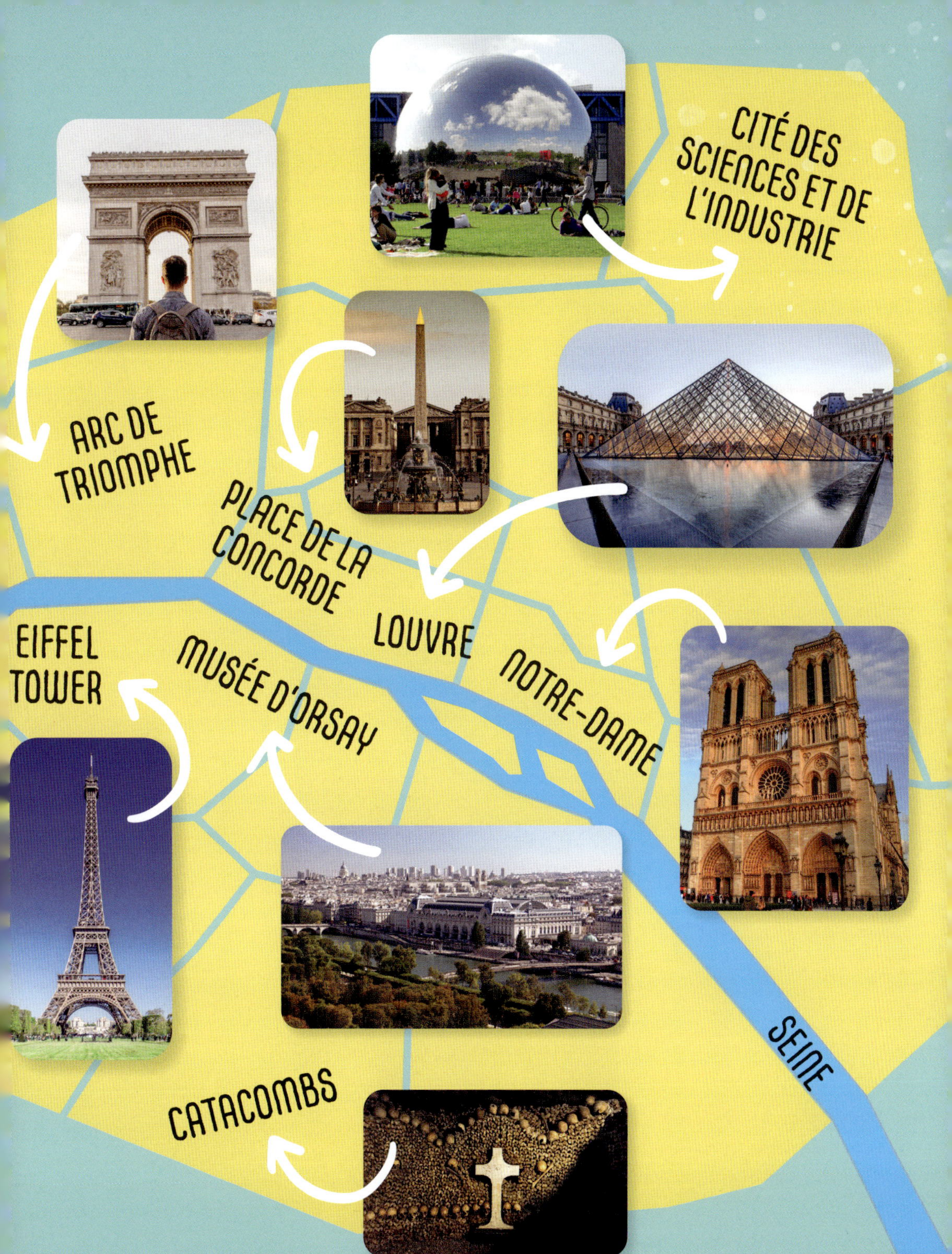

CITÉ DES SCIENCES ET DE L'INDUSTRIE

ARC DE TRIOMPHE

PLACE DE LA CONCORDE

LOUVRE

NOTRE-DAME

EIFFEL TOWER

MUSÉE D'ORSAY

SEINE

CATACOMBS

Mapping It Out 15

Meet the Metro

With 16 lines and more than 300 stations, the Paris metro is bustling. It's also one of the world's oldest metros, and its stations are very unique. The Arts et Métiers stop (below) is designed to look like a submarine!

Fast Facts

Average distance from station to station: **457 m (1,500 ft)**

Number of Paris neighbourhoods: **20**

Deepest stop: **Abbesses station; 36 m (118 ft)**

IMAGES: Arts et Métiers metro station (left); cyclists reading a map (above).

GETTING AROUND TOWN

ALLONS-Y!

IMAGE: The entrance to the Parmentier metro station.

ON THE WATER

CRUISE THE SEINE

It could be said that the **Seine River** is the heart of Paris. It has been used by people to come and go for centuries – Paris was founded more than 2,000 years ago. During the ninth century, Vikings rowed their swift longboats up the Seine and attacked Paris three different times! Today, the river is one of the best ways to see the city. You can hop on a river bus or take a river cruise while you have a bite to eat.

In 1910, the Seine flooded so much that Parisians had to get around the entire city by boat!

Fast Facts

Hours of operation:
10 a.m. to 7 p.m.

Number of seats:
180

Passes available for:
1 or 2 days

BOARD THE BATOBUS

All aboard! The Batobus is a bus – er, boat – that travels the Seine and allows passengers to hop on and off at nine different stops around the city. Much more casual than a cruise, the Batobus lets passengers create their own journeys and exit the river to explore the city for as long as they want – then hop back on. Stops include some of the city's most famous sights, such as Notre-Dame Cathedral (see pages 50-51), the Louvre (see pages 52-53), and much more. Sightseeing, ahoy!

IMAGES: The Pont Neuf over the Seine (above); passengers boarding the Batobus (left).

Getting Around Town 21

HITTING THE ROAD

CALL A CAB

Zip through the streets in a taxi, which you can flag down at a taxi stand. Like the famous yellow taxis of New York City, you can tell if a taxi is available if the light on top is lit up. Green means hop right in! Red means the taxi is taken. Unlike New York taxis, Parisian taxis are usually all black!

The first 'buses' in Paris included a system of horse-drawn carriages created back in the early 1600s.

BEEP BEEP!

Do you want to travel like many of the locals do? Hop on one of the many buses around Paris. Just make sure to have your bus ticket to hand, which can be purchased at a metro station, newsstand or on the bus. For sightseeing, board one of the red buses designed with visitors and tourists in mind: these make loops of some of the more famous sites, providing fun facts along the way.

START YOUR CARTS

If you're looking to hit the streets on wheels but want something a little more unique, consider taking a golf-cart tour. These small, open-air carts let you zoom around the city while taking in the sights in style. Best of all, the golf carts are electric: they're fun and eco-friendly, too!

IMAGES: Golf cart, Tuileries Garden (left); Arc de Triomphe on the Champs-Élysées (below); Parisian bus stop (opposite bottom); taxi (opposite top).

AFTER DARK

Many Paris bus lines stop running in the evenings. Need to travel late at night? Never fear – the Noctilien is here! The night buses in Paris run from around midnight to early morning and connect with major train stations to make getting around a snap.

ON THE METRO

Trains on the Paris metro run about 966,000 km (600,000 miles) per day – that's 24 times around the globe!

IMAGES: A metro entrance from the early 20th century (below); metro musicians (opposite top).

If you're searching for the quickest and easiest way to get around town, consider going underground – on the Paris metro.

Paris metro stations are famous for their fancy entrances that date back to the metro's early days. Today, the system seems super hi-tech – almost futuristic – as it whizzes deep under the city. But the metro isn't new; the very first lines under Paris opened in 1900.

Workers dug deep into the earth to remove mountains of rubble. There, they placed enormous metal tunnels. Then they placed train tracks along the tunnels. It was an engineering marvel. After the first stations opened, Parisians were eager to hop on the new trains. Today, people take 1.5 billion trips on the Paris metro each year.

There are more than 300 stations – and 12 ghost stations, which are completely abandoned. The Gare de Lyon station includes an underground tropical garden, and Châtelet-Les Halles is the largest metro station in the world!

METRO MUSICIANS

What is the greatest stage in Paris? According to some, it's the metro! Twice a year, scores of musicians audition to become metro musicians, or performers who play in the Paris metro stations. Each year, the city hosts 300 musicians who are chosen to reflect the many different musical styles of Paris and its citizens.

TRAVEL BY FOOT

STROLL THE STREETS

One of the best ways to get around Paris is on foot! The city is made up of wide-open boulevards and winding, narrow streets. Strolling on foot gives you close-up views of everything from fancy streetlamps and cool carvings on buildings to hidden cafés for a quick snack stop. Just be sure to bring comfortable shoes: many streets are made from cobblestones, and others are hilly. Paris has always been a walking city. In fact, a 3.6-km (2.25-mile) moving sidewalk was built for the 1900 Exposition Universelle (see page 78) to help people get around. Called the 'wooden serpent', it was built 9 m (30 ft) above the ground!

Fast Facts

Amount of bike lanes: **more than 1,000 km (620 miles)**, equal to about the length of all of France

Number of bike parking stands: **60,000**

Vélib' bikes are recycled into new items once they are no longer usable. Old inner tubes are turned into bags, and tires are turned into belts!

BIKES OR BUST

It's an iconic Parisian image: bicycle riders pedalling through the city streets with a baguette tucked into their bike basket. Bicycles are super popular in Paris. In fact, there are more bike riders than car drivers in the city! Bike lanes are everywhere, making it easier for cyclists to get around. Many riders use bike-sharing services, like Vélib', which allows cyclists to pick up one of their 19,000 bicycles – including electric bikes – pedal away, and then drop off the bicycle at one of more than 1,400 stands.

The first Sunday of each month is a car-free day when parts of Paris close access to cars.

IMAGES: Saint Gervais Church, Le Marais (above); the Seine (left).

Getting Around Town 27

ON THE RAILS

What's the difference between a tram and a train? Also sometimes called a trolley, a tram is a type of train that runs on aboveground tracks. It's powered by electricity, often through the cables that run above it.

Fast Facts

Number of tram routes: **13**

Number of stations: **more than 250**

Year the first trams ran in Paris: **1853**

TRAM TIME

Trams, trains, river tours and more – there is no shortage of ways to get around Paris! The first trams in the city were pulled by horses. In the 1800s, there was a large network of electric trams that lasted until the late 1950s. The last tram line in this network went to the Palace of Versailles and made its last trip in 1957. By the late 20th century, trams were back in business as a clean and green way to get around town.

EXPRESS STOP

Paris's RER, or Réseau Express Régional, is the city's express train. In other words, it's fast! Within the city, it can go up to 100 km/h (62 mph). The RER makes fewer stops, so what would be a 30-minute journey on the metro takes only 10 minutes on the RER! It's the perfect way to get to major sites, including Disneyland Paris (see pages 38-39) and Versailles (see pages 84-85).

France is developing high-speed 'drone trains' that will drive themselves.

ALL ABOARD!

The Transilien is a regional train that takes passengers from the centre of the city to the farther reaches of Paris. The train first opened in 1837. Today, it carries tens of thousands of people each week! It's the busiest train network in the world after Tokyo's train system when it comes to the number of passengers it carries.

IMAGES: A Paris tram (opposite); the RER Invalides station (above); Gare Saint-Lazare train station (left).

Getting Around Town 29

AN UNUSUAL RIDE

What's fun and a little bit peculiar? The funicular! (Okay, the word 'funicular' doesn't actually come from those two words.) It's a type of cable train used to go up and down mountainsides – like the **Montmartre funicular**.

Montmartre is a neighbourhood located on a hill. It has great views, but it can be hard to hike to the top (see pages 100-101). Instead, you can hop aboard the funicular, which has been operating for more than 100 years.

The funicular was originally powered by water. The cars were grouped in pairs attached by a long cable. Each car was mounted with a water tank that was filled or emptied, depending on how many people were in the car. Cars going down the hill had their tanks filled with water to help them descend. This would also help the car 'push' the other one up the hill! In 1935, the funicular switched to electricity. The cars still help each other move, but their motion is created by a motor. They scale the mountain in less than two minutes!

IMAGE: *The Montmartre funicular.*

A city in the south of France once had a cable car that travelled underwater.

FUNICULAR FUN
The highest funicular, built along a mountainside in Switzerland, takes riders 1,300 m (4,265 ft) up – more than four times the height of the Eiffel Tower!

PLACES TO PLAY

IMAGE: A roller coaster at Parc Astérix.

ÇA C'EST COOL!

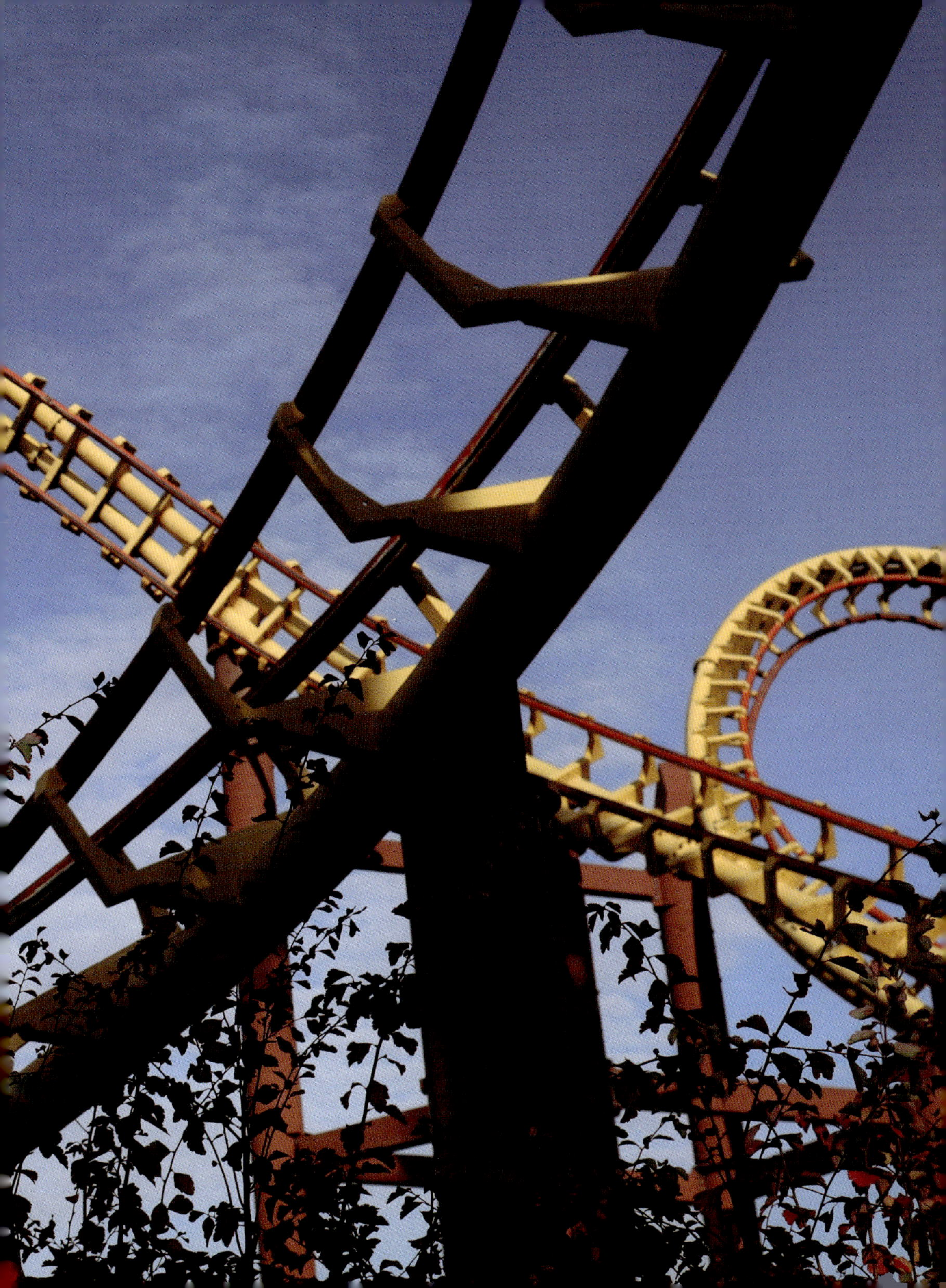

GET HANDS-ON

LIGHT UP THE CITY
A former factory might not sound like the perfect place to play – but just wait until the lights go on! Built in 1835, this historic building now houses the **Atelier des Lumières**: an interactive museum of lights. Wander the halls as enormous projections make it seem like you've been transported to another place. Scenes include travels back in time, explorations deep under the ocean, journeys inside your favourite painting – and much more.

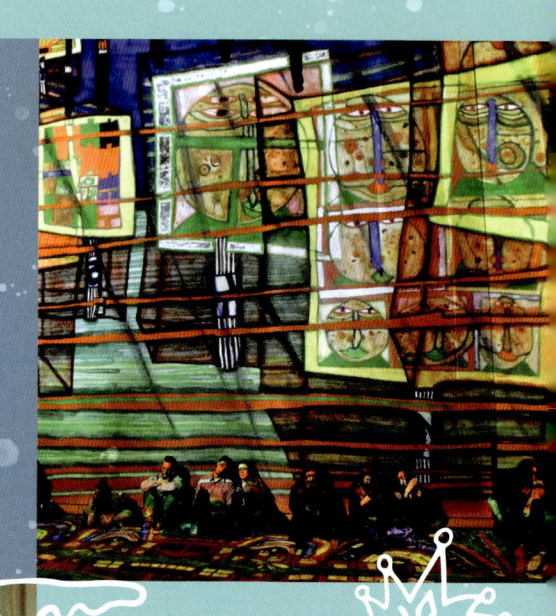

WACKY WAX
Want to meet your favourite actor, singer or even cartoon character? Then head to the **Musée Grévin** (Grévin Museum), which features lifelike wax statues of some of the most famous figures of all time. Pose with sports superstars or travel back in time to meet kings and queens. You can even go behind the scenes to learn how the museum has been creating their ultra-realistic wax figures for more than 135 years.

One wax figure can use more than 34 kg (75 lb) of wax – and thousands of real hairs!

CAROUSEL COLLECTION

If you're a fan of fairs and festivals, you won't want to miss the **Musée des Arts Forains** (Fairground Museum). The museum was started by Jean Paul Favand, who dedicated his life to collecting historic fairground rides and attractions. Thanks to cutting-edge technologies, visitors today can not only learn about the history of carnivals, but actually ride the rides!

IMAGES: Digital art at the Atelier des Lumières (opposite top); a vintage carousel at Musée des Arts Forains (left); an Omnimax theatre at Cité des Sciences et de l'Industrie (below); a wax figure of France's King Louis XIV at Musée Grévin (opposite bottom).

Historians think that the carousel ride may have been based on a game from the 12th century in which horseback riders tossed a ball to one another.

SUPER SCIENCE

Boost your brain and get creative at **Cité des Sciences et de l'Industrie**, a science museum that lets you experiment with sound, study robots or climb aboard a real historic submarine. If that's not enough activity for you, head to the Cité des Enfants. Designed just for kids, this part of the museum has games, interactive science experiments, learning stations and even obstacle courses.

PRIME PARKS

FIELD OF FOLLIES

Parc de la Villette is enormous! It's a popular spot for festivals, outdoor movies, sports games and more. The park contains 26 red mini buildings, or follies, each featuring a different attraction, and it's the perfect place to dash around at a playground, see a concert or discover something new – the park is home to Europe's largest science museum!

Long ago, the area that is now Parc de la Villette was home to a large meat market.

TAME A DRAGON

Jardin du Dragon might be located within Parc de la Villette, but this playground is a beast of its own. As the name suggests, the playground is shaped like an enormous dragon, and it stretches 25 m (92 ft) – that's about the length of a blue whale. Scale the dragon's body using ropes, nets and stairs, and then zip down a long, metal tube slide – the dragon's tongue!

IMAGES: The slide at Jardin du Dragon (left); a folly at Parc de la Villette (above); Luxembourg Palace and its gardens (opposite top); the swing carousel at Jardin d'Acclimatation (opposite bottom).

FEELING FANCY?

Located outside of the famed Palais du Luxembourg (see page 87), **Jardin du Luxembourg** is vast. Bright green lawns and colourful flowers are in every direction. Here, enjoy a puppet show, pony rides and a playground. Then take part in toy boat races in the pond. Want to see pups at play? A dog park allows our four-legged friends to frolic to their hearts' content.

> A miniature version of the Statue of Liberty sits in Jardin du Luxembourg. New York's Lady Liberty was a gift from France to the US.

GET YOUR THRILLS

Calling all thrill-seekers: **Jardin d'Acclimatation** is part garden, part amusement park. Take a spin on the swing ride, scream your lungs out on the tower drop, or take your pick of several roller coasters. If you're feeling more low-key, check out the petting zoos or fabulous fountains. The park even hosts concerts, dance performances, circuses and lantern festivals.

Places to Play 37

FOR YOUR AMUSEMENT

BLAST FROM THE PAST

Just north of the city, discover an adventure land that lets you journey back in time to visit the ancient Gauls (people of ancient France), Romans, Greeks, Egyptians, Vikings and more. Even better – you'll be doing loop-the-loops on roller coasters and splashing down water rides as you go! **Parc Astérix** is an amusement park featuring some 50 attractions sure to delight all thrill-seekers. Look for two stars of the park: Toutatis, the highest and fastest roller coaster in the country, and Goudurix, a coaster with seven upside-down turns!

Fast Facts

Number of rides at Disneyland Paris: **54**

Visitors per year: **9.9 million**

Size: **57 hectares (140 acres)**

Toutatis reaches 51 m (167 ft) high and clocks speeds of up to 110 km/h (68 mph)!

MEET THE STARS

Do you know what else Paris can claim? It's home to one of the happiest places on Earth! Journey east of the city to reach **Disneyland Paris**, where you'll find rides, restaurants, games, shows and more, all inspired by popular characters from Disney, Star Wars, Marvel, and Pixar. Plus, enjoy meet and greets with the stars of your favourite films. Then, head next door to the Walt Disney Studios Park. Here, you can catch more spine-tingling rides and learn how some of your favourite films were made.

Disneyland 'employs' around 200 cats who help keep the grounds free from pesky rodents.

IMAGES: The Goudurix roller coaster at Parc Astérix (above); Disneyland Hotel (left).

Places to Play 39

SHOWTIME!

GO GRAND

If you're looking for a show, there's no better venue than **Palais Garnier**. In fact, the building itself is quite a show! Built in 1861, the opera house features enormous carved pillars, towering domes, golden statues and a grand staircase. It took 14 years to complete the brilliant building. The golden walls and red velvet seats are set beneath a painted ceiling and a gigantic chandelier – it weighs 7 tonnes (8 tons) and has 340 lights! Here, visitors can catch operas, ballets, concerts and other performances amid all the grandeur.

HAUNTED HAPPENINGS

During one show in 1896, the enormous chandelier at Palais Garnier mysteriously fell from the ceiling. Inspired by the accident, author Gaston Leroux went on to write his famous horror novel, *The Phantom of the Opera*, about an opera house haunted by a menacing man known as the Phantom. Leroux also took inspiration from the Palais Garnier's many hidden passageways and tunnels (although there was never a real phantom!).

MUSIC TO YOUR EARS

Whether you visit Paris in the heat of summer or the chilly winter, **Philharmonie de Paris** is a must-see. The symphony hall is famous for its glittering silver exterior, which is covered in 340,000 aluminum birds that look like they are taking flight! There are about 500 concerts each year, so you're sure to catch a great show here. From rock to jazz to classical music to hip-hop, the concert hall features music of all kinds.

Fast Facts

Number of seats in Philharmonie de Paris: **2,400**

Opening year: **2015**

Musicians in the orchestra: **around 119**

IMAGES: Inside Palais Garnier (above); Philharmonie de Paris's famous exterior (left).

Places to Play 41

GAME ON

Sports fans can kick things off with a game at the largest stadium in France. **Stade de France** was originally built for the 1998 FIFA World Cup, an international football tournament. The stadium is so large that the roof alone weighs 1.5 times the weight of the Eiffel Tower! With seating for 80,000 people, the stadium also hosts rugby games and track-and-field events. But it isn't just for sports; the stadium hosts some of the most famous musical artists in the world, such as Beyoncé and Taylor Swift.

In 2024, Stade de France was one of dozens of venues in and around Paris to host the Olympic and Paralympic Games. The stadium added an athletics track for track-and-field events, and the entire city adjusted to host the Summer Games! To accommodate visitors, city officials installed 55 km (34 miles) of new bike routes and began building four new metro lines and a whopping 68 new stations.

Breaking, or breakdancing – a type of acrobatic dance which originated in New York City – became an Olympic sport for the first time at the Paris 2024 Summer Olympics.

IMAGES: Inside Stade de France (right); Parkour (opposite).

42   A Kid's Guide to PARIS

STREET SPORTS

Paris's arenas and stadiums are home to some of the city's most impressive sports tournaments, but many Parisian sports also take place on the streets – such as skateboarding, breakdancing and parkour. In fact, parkour first originated in France in the 1980s. In parkour, athletes use urban surroundings and human-made structures as obstacle courses.

WHAT A VIEW!

IMAGE: Paris at sunset.

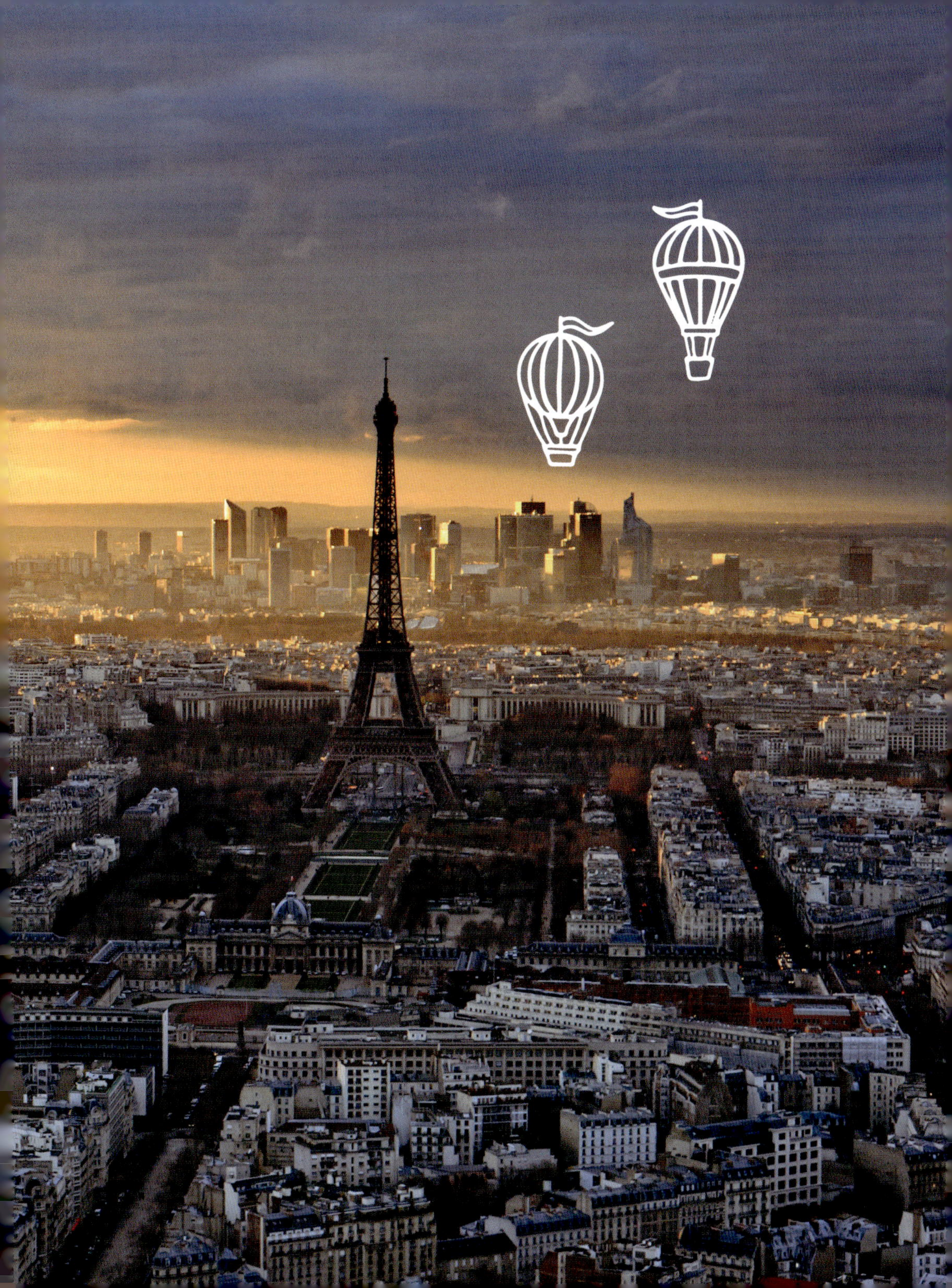

THE EIFFEL TOWER

The **Eiffel Tower** was originally built for the Exposition Universelle, a world's fair held in 1889. It was a victory of engineering. On top of using scaffolds and cranes, construction workers created a foundation of concrete under the earth. This included parts of the Seine River: there, they sank large watertight containers into the river, which allowed them to work while keeping out the water.

As well as looking good, the tower made waves for another reason: it was the first structure in the world to reach 305 m (1,000 ft). Today, it remains as famous as ever: more than seven million visitors come to see the iron tower each year.

The tippy-top of the Eiffel Tower is one of the best places to view Paris. But what about viewing the tower itself? Most fans agree that the **Jardins du Trocadéro** on the opposite side of the river offers the most picture-perfect glimpses. Here, the sight of the Eiffel Tower will make you feel like you just stepped out of a painting.

IMAGES: Eiffel Tower along the Seine (right); below the Eiffel Tower (opposite).

46 A Kid's Guide to PARIS

Over the years, the Eiffel Tower has been painted various shades of red, yellow and brown.

TOUR THE TOWER

Gustave Eiffel, who designed the Eiffel Tower, built an office at the top of the tower to conduct science experiments. It can still be seen today. Visitors can also find shops and restaurants inside the tower, including Le Jules Verne – named after the famous French writer – where diners can take in city views.

BIRD'S-EYE VIEW

UP, UP, AND AWAY

Flying isn't just for the birds! Get a unique view of Paris – and a thrill – when you glide above the city in a hot-air balloon. The **Ballon de Paris Generali** (Generali Balloon of Paris), the world's largest hot-air balloon, takes riders up to a height of 150 m (500 ft) and over some of the city's most well-known landmarks.

Generali becomes a floating laboratory when in flight, collecting air quality data for the city and displaying its findings inside the balloon.

A WILD RIDE

In 1783, two French brothers launched the first ever hot-air balloon south of Paris in Annonay, France, complete with passengers. However, the riders weren't people. They included a rooster, a duck and a sheep! The trip was a success: all animals (and the balloon) returned safely.

A French daredevil named Alain Robert climbed up the outside of Montparnasse Tower in 2015.

DO LOOK DOWN

When **Montparnasse Tower** was completed in 1973, it caused quite a stir. Many people felt that it didn't fit in with Paris's other buildings, or that its design was unappealing. Today, at 210 m (689 ft), the tower is still central Paris's only skyscraper, and it remains a bit controversial. But one thing Parisians (and visitors) can agree on is that the views from Montparnasse Tower are fantastic. With a 360-degree observation deck, the tower offers a breathtaking panorama of the city.

IMAGES: Ballon de Paris Generali (above); the view from Montparnasse Tower's observation deck (left).

What a View! 49

NOTRE-DAME CATHEDRAL

About 13 million people visit Notre-Dame each year.

GO GOTHIC

Cathédrale Notre-Dame de Paris (Notre-Dame Cathedral) looks like something out of a medieval fairy tale – because it is! Construction on the cathedral began in the 12th century on Paris's Île de la Cité, an island in the Seine (see pages 112-113). The building took 300 years to complete, but it was more than worth it: with its stained-glass windows, delicate stonework and towering spires, Notre-Dame is a sight to behold. In 2019, a massive fire almost destroyed the cathedral forever. Restoration efforts quickly got underway, and today it remains one of the most famous cathedrals in the world.

IMAGES: A side view of Notre-Dame Cathedral before the fire (above); a Notre-Dame grotesque above the city (opposite top); the entrance to the Crypte Archéologique in the Notre-Dame plaza (opposite bottom).

50 A Kid's Guide to PARIS

How Grotesque!

While you're here, don't miss the amazing views from inside Notre-Dame, too. Get a glimpse of the enormous organ and stunning stained-glass rose windows, and then head to the towers for fantastic views of the surrounding city. You'll be in good company: perched on Notre-Dame are dozens of gargoyles and grotesques. Both are stone carvings made to resemble dragons, fierce animals and monsters. What's the difference? Gargoyles serve as waterspouts to direct rainfall away from the building, while grotesques are just for decoration.

Some of the Notre-Dame grotesques have nicknames: one is known as 'the vampire'.

View the Past

Notre-Dame may be the most famous building on Île de la Cité, but it was not the first. Roughly 2,000 years ago, the site belonged to an ancient Roman temple. Get a glimpse into the ancient past at the **Crypte Archéologique** (Archaeological Crypt), a museum set beneath – as in, underground – Notre-Dame. There, you'll see ancient Gallo-Roman and medieval ruins.

What a View! 51

LOTS TO LOUVRE

Today, the **Musée du Louvre** (Louvre Museum) is the most visited art museum or gallery in the world. But in the 12th century, it was the site of a royal fortress. In the 16th century, that building was destroyed to make way for the structure that remains today. This complex was used as a palace for France's kings until the 17th century, eventually becoming a museum in 1793. Now it houses more than 500,000 pieces.

At the end of the 20th century, the Louvre was expanded to make room for more masterpieces. As part of the renovations, the architect I. M. Pei designed an enormous glass courtyard for the museum's new entrance.

There's a good chance you've heard of the *Mona Lisa*. After all, it's one of the most famous paintings in the world. Now is your chance to get a close-up view. Painted in the early 1500s by Leonardo da Vinci, the *Mona Lisa* is known for the subject's mysterious smile and almost hypnotic gaze.

IMAGES: Pyramide du Louvre, the main entrance to the Louvre Museum (right); the *Mona Lisa* (opposite).

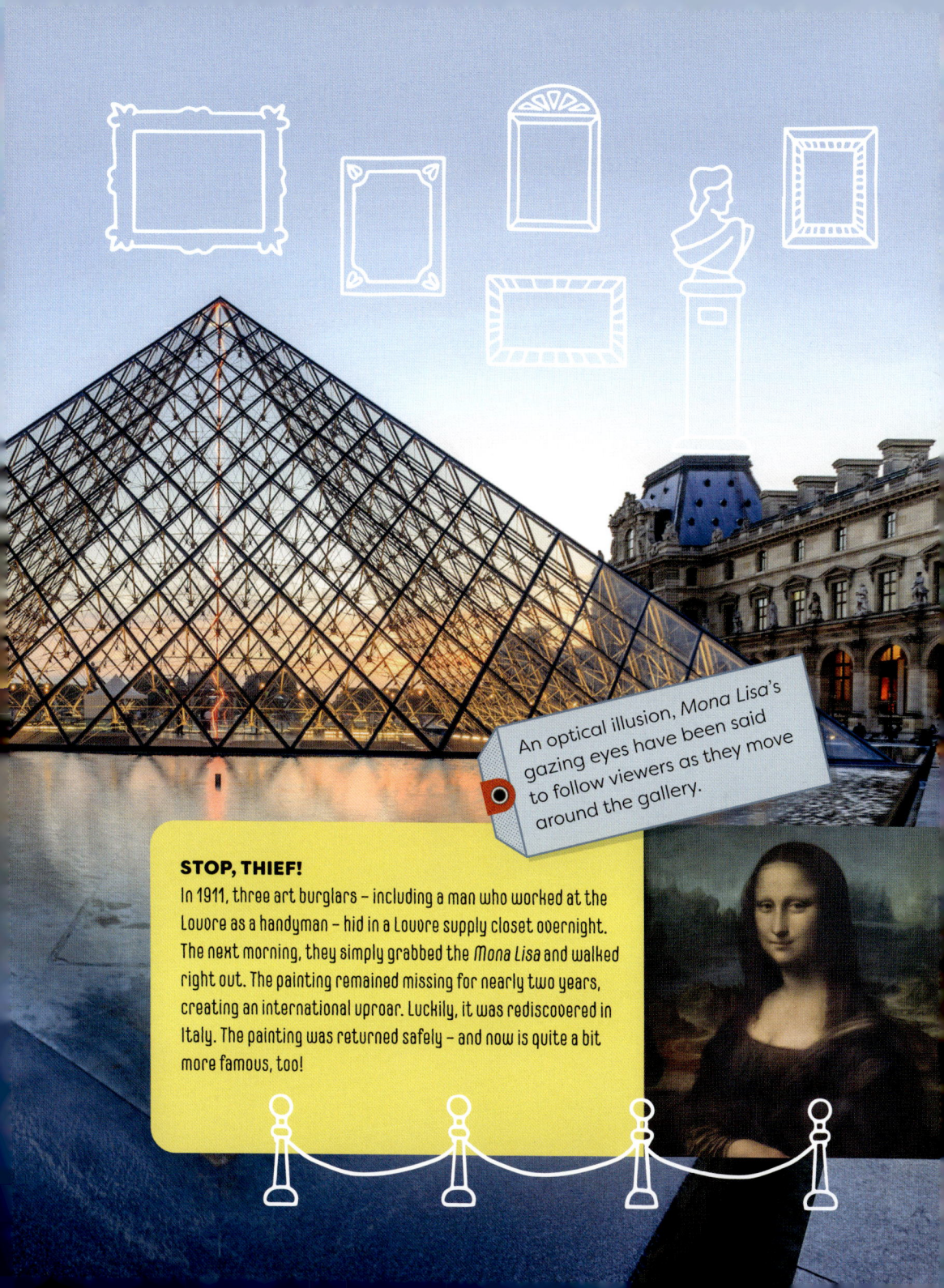

An optical illusion, Mona Lisa's gazing eyes have been said to follow viewers as they move around the gallery.

STOP, THIEF!
In 1911, three art burglars – including a man who worked at the Louvre as a handyman – hid in a Louvre supply closet overnight. The next morning, they simply grabbed the *Mona Lisa* and walked right out. The painting remained missing for nearly two years, creating an international uproar. Luckily, it was rediscovered in Italy. The painting was returned safely – and now is quite a bit more famous, too!

AT THE MUSÉE D'ORSAY

SECRET SIGHTS

Opened in the 1980s, the **Musée d'Orsay** (Orsay Museum) holds some of the world's greatest French artistic masterpieces. However, the building also contains a secret: visitors who make the trek to the top floors will find incredible views of the city. First, peek out at Paris through the enormous clockface. Next, head to the roof balcony for a sweeping – and uncrowded – glimpse of the city below.

PAINTING PARADISE

The Musée d'Orsay contains mainly 19th-century Impressionist art by French artists. Impressionism was a type of painting style and technique that was shared by a group of artists at the same time. Impressionist painters painted a reflection, or impression, of real life. You get to see what light, an object, a person or a landscape looked like through their eyes.

IMAGES: Visitors at the Musée d'Orsay admire Renoir's Bal du moulin de la Galette *(left)*; inside the Musée d'Orsay's clockface *(top)*; Main Hall, Musée d'Orsay *(opposite top)*; Musée d'Orsay and the Seine River *(opposite bottom)*.

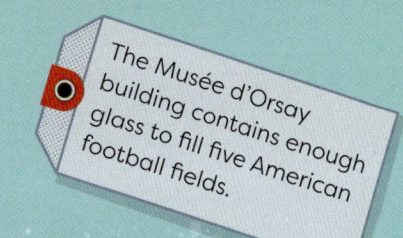

The Musée d'Orsay building contains enough glass to fill five American football fields.

SUBLIME SCULPTURE

The centre of the Musée d'Orsay was a railway station originally built in 1900. Today, it houses a top-tier collection of statues, most of which were created by French artists. Whether made of stone or metal, the statues look so real, it seems they might come to life!

FANTASTIC PHOTOS

It may come as a surprise that – as a museum that houses art mainly from the 19th century – the Musée d'Orsay features a photography collection. As photography was first invented in the 1830s, the museum holds some of the oldest surviving photographs. Peer into the past with photos that capture how the world looked nearly two centuries ago.

There are more than 130 museums in Paris.

LET'S EAT!

IMAGE: Croissants

BREAD AND CHEESE

BEHOLD THE BAGUETTE

The baguette is a long, thin loaf of bread. Crusty on the outside and soft on the inside, it is perfect for slicing or tearing apart with your hands – and easy to transport. No one is sure who first invented the baguette. However, it became very popular during World War II, when France was under occupation by foreign countries. The bread served as a sign of French resistance and culture. Each year, a competition is held in Paris to find the city's best baguette!

THE PERFECT PASTRY

Delightfully light and flaky, the croissant is a buttery pastry rolled up into a crescent shape. It is commonly eaten plain or with jam – however, many bakeries also sell croissants stuffed with chocolate or sweet almond paste. Though the croissant is a famous French pastry, its origins actually come from a curved Austrian pastry known as the kipferl.

IMAGES: A flaky croissant (left); fresh baguettes (above); an assortment of Brie and other French cheeses (opposite top); Roquefort cheese with pears and nuts (opposite bottom).

PASS THE BRIE

Mmm . . . rich, creamy, and soft, Brie is sometimes thought of as one of the most luxurious cheeses on Earth. However, its origins are much humbler: historians think Brie was first created by French monks in the seventh century. Try spreading it on a warm baguette – or if you're feeling adventurous, try it with fruit!

> The firm outer shell, or rind, on Brie is actually a harmless mould like that in Roquefort.

MORE CHEESE, PLEASE!

Get ready for Roquefort, a type of blue cheese – that is, a cheese that contains harmless, edible mould – made in Roquefort in the south of France. This cheese has been eaten since at least the 1300s, and it became so popular that in 1411, it was granted official royal protection by King Charles VI. Roquefort has a strong, sharp salty taste – and a stronger smell!

TIME FOR LUNCH

BETTER WITH BUTTER

What do you get when you combine some of the most iconic French foods into the perfect sandwich? A jambon-beurre! Perfect for eating on the go, this simple sandwich is named for its star ingredients: a type of sliced ham known as Jambon de Paris and unsalted butter, which are layered onto a sliced baguette. Want to take it to the next level? Add some creamy Camembert cheese!

IMAGES: Jambon-beurre (above); croque monsieurs, a croque madame, fries and salad (opposite top); sweet crêpes with raspberries and chocolate (opposite bottom).

GET GRILLING

Calling all fans of toasted cheese sandwiches: things are about to get wild. Unlike the cheese toasties you know, a croque monsieur is made with rich, melty Gruyère cheese. And on this sandwich, the cheese is on the outside! A croque monsieur features ham and a creamy, butter-based Béchamel sauce between two thick slices of bread. Cheese is then placed on top of the sandwich, and the whole thing is grilled until the cheese is gooey and warm.

A croque madame is a croque monsieur with a fried egg on top.

In France, 2 February is La Chandeleur (also known as Candlemas), a holiday dedicated to eating crêpes.

SWEET AND SAVOURY

According to lore, crêpes were invented sometime in the 13th century when a home baker in northern France accidentally spilled porridge onto a hot stove. The porridge turned nice and crispy, forming a thin pancake. Today, crêpes come in many styles and with even more fillings. Is it lunchtime? Try a savoury crêpe (known as a galette) filled with cheese, vegetables, eggs and more. Want a sweet treat? Grab one stuffed with chocolate sauce, whipped cream and fruit. You can't go wrong!

Let's Eat! 61

ON THE MENU

SOUP'S ON

In a country famous for its culinary creations and unique cooking methods, one standout is rich, flavourful French onion soup. The soup is made using caramelised onions, which are yellow onions that have been slowly cooked until they turn sweet. Then, a thick wedge of bread is stuffed into the soup and topped with magnificent, melty cheese. Versions of French onion soup have been beloved in France for nearly 1,000 years. Made with easily found ingredients, the soup was popular among the working class. However, thanks to its delicious flavours, it was also a huge hit with kings and nobles!

Ratatouille, a vegetable stew from southern France, is so popular that it is featured in the animated Pixar film *Ratatouille*.

FAMOUS FRIES

French fries are famous around the world – but the way they are eaten changes from place to place! In France, kids often dip their frites (fries) in ketchup and mayo. In Vietnam, fries are given a flavourful combo of butter and sugar. And in Québec, Canada, people enjoy poutine: a dish of French fries smothered in brown gravy sauce and topped with cheese curds. Bon appétit!

MAIN MEALS

What should you order when at a French bistro, or casual restaurant? One of France's most famous dishes is steak frites (steak with a side of French fries). The meal is often served plain or *au poivre*: doused in a rich pepper sauce. For those who don't eat meat, there are plenty of veggies to go around. Consider a vegetarian quiche – a savoury pastry filled with a custard-like mixture made from eggs and cream. You'll also find a wide variety of savoury tarts filled with seasonal vegetables and local cheeses.

IMAGES: Ratatouille (left); French onion soup (opposite top); fries with mayonnaise (above).

Let's Eat! 63

SUPERB SWEETS

BEST OF THE BREST

If you need a dessert for a special occasion, the Paris-Brest is the choice for you. This impressive sweet features two rings of delicate-but-crispy choux pastry sandwiching a thick, custard-like cream. This cream, known as crème mousseline, often has a sugary, nutty flavour called praline. The whole thing is then topped with slivered almonds.

EXCELLENT ÉCLAIRS

Perhaps the most popular of all the French pastries, the éclair is a dessert made of a light and crispy dough. The dough is then filled with cream or custard and topped with a shiny glaze flavoured with anything from chocolate to caramel to passion fruit and more. The name 'éclair' means 'flash of lightning' – possibly because the pastry is so good that it is gone in a flash!

IMAGES: An assortment of éclairs (left); Paris-Brests with chocolate and custard fillings (above); Opéra cakes (opposite top); strawberry-flavoured mille-feuille (opposite bottom).

TAKE THE CAKE

With seven layers of perfection, the Opéra cake is as grand as a musical performance. Unlike many pastries with ancient histories, the Opéra cake is a relatively recent innovation: it is believed to have been created in the 1950s. With seven layers of sponge cake, coffee cream and shiny chocolate ganache, the dessert gained icon status almost immediately!

The St Honoré is named for the French patron saint of bakers.

PASTRY PARTY

There are so many terrific Parisian treats, it can be hard to decide on the perfect pastry – but you can't go wrong with these two classic French creations. Famed for its many flaky layers, the mille-feuille is made of three tiers of puff pastry stacked on top of thick custard cream and decorated with a layer of icing glaze. Like the mille-feuille, the St Honoré also features delicate puff pastry; but it is shaped into a ring, topped with crème-filled pastry balls covered in caramelised sugar, and smothered in pastry cream.

Let's Eat! 65

SNAIL SNACKING

Depending on where you're from, you might hesitate at the idea of slurping down a snail. But in France, snails are considered a delicacy. Here, edible snails are known as escargots.

Snacking on snails isn't anything new; some of the first stories of dining on snails come from the ancient Romans more than 2,000 years ago. But humans have probably been eating them longer than that: there is evidence that ancient humans were eating snails more than 30,000 years ago! However, according to legend, escargots as we know them developed in the 17th century under the reign of King Louis XIV – but no one knows for sure!

So, what are they like? To serve escargots the French way, the snails are briefly boiled without their shells. They are then cooked in a mixture of garlic butter and herbs and served back in their shells. Diners use a special small fork to remove the meat from the shell and then – down the hatch! Fans describe escargot as tasting similar to a mix between clams and mushrooms.

Escargots are meant to be chewed – in fact, they're often a bit chewy.

IMAGES: Escargots (right); L'Escargot Montorgueil (opposite).

CENTURIES OF SNAILS

Eager to eat some escargot? Try L'Escargot Montorgueil, a historic eatery that serves snails and has been operating since 1832. The entranceway is even topped with a giant golden snail!

Let's Eat! 67

GLOBAL GRUB

MERCI!

French food has influenced cuisine around the world: in New York, one pastry chef invented a cross between the doughnut and croissant known as a Cronut.

FALAFEL FEAST

France is a country of strong French tradition and culture – but it is also a city of multicultural influences. Thanks to many immigrants from Lebanon and Syria, Paris boasts some of the best falafel in the world. Falafel are deep-fried patties or balls made of chickpeas or fava beans. They are often eaten with flavourful sauces like hummus or tahini and commonly served in warm flatbreads called pita.

IMAGES: Falafel with pita and yoghurt dip (above); tagine (opposite top); bánh mì sandwich (opposite bottom).

68   A Kid's Guide to PARIS

TAGINE TIME

Tagine is a rich, slow-cooked stew named for the uniquely shaped clay pots used to make the dish. Though it comes from countries across North Africa, authentic tagine can also be found throughout Paris. Beginning in the early 20th century, many people from Morocco and other parts of North Africa began to immigrate to France. As they moved, they brought many of their customs with them – including tagine, which quickly became a hit all over the country.

FOOD FUSION

During the 19th century, French colonisers invaded parts of Southeast Asia, including Vietnam. This led to quite a bit of French influence on parts of Vietnamese culture and daily life – and vice versa. One such example of cultural fusion was the bánh mì, a baguette sandwich filled with grilled meats, pickled vegetables and Vietnamese sauces. More recently, bò bún has become super popular in Paris. This dish features chilled rice noodles, pickled veggies, grilled meats and lemongrass sauces. Yum!

Let's Eat! 69

STROLL THE CHAMPS-ÉLYSÉES

IMAGE: View of the Arc de Triomphe from the Champs-Élysées.

LIFE OF LUXURY

TRÈS CHIC

One of the city's major avenues, the **Champs-Élysées** got its start in the early 17th century, when it was fashioned into an avenue of trees for Queen Marie de Médicis. Soon, boutiques and shops began to open along the boulevard, and by the 1800s, it was seen as one of the most fashionable spots in the city. Today, the Champs-Élysées has become a top destination for tourists in Paris, as well as the home of many world-famous luxury brands.

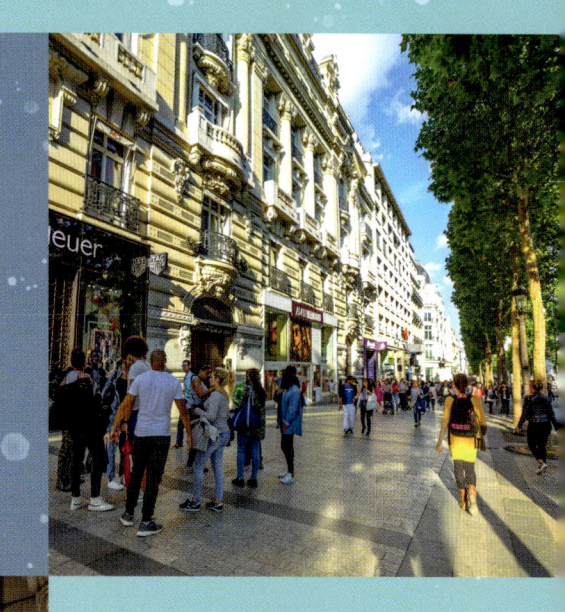

FOLLOW YOUR NOSE

Fashion is far from the only luxury available on the Champs-Élysées. Follow the sweet scents to **Guerlain**, a famous perfumery that first opened in 1828. Guerlain was responsible for supplying unique perfumes to the rich and famous, including the wife of French emperor Napoleon III.

Marvellous Macarons

Can a cookie be luxurious? It can if it comes from **Ladurée**! This fashionable pastry house was first created in 1862. In 1930, Ladurée became the birthplace of the most iconic of French cookies: the macaron. They are so popular in France that 20 March is national macaron day. Light as air, these classic cookie sandwiches are made of almond flour and meringue – whipped egg whites – and stuffed with flavoured filling. Most macarons are brightly coloured, making them (almost!) too pretty to eat. From rose to chocolate to pistachio, macarons come in endless flavours. Stop in for an afternoon treat!

Classic Bites

On the Champs-Élysées is **Brasserie Fouquet's**, a historic French brasserie (a casual eatery). First opened at this spot in 1899, the eatery is very fancy! It offers French classics like steak tartare (raw beef chopped finely and often served with a raw egg yolk) and the famous French escargots (see pages 66-67).

IMAGES: Guerlain storefront (opposite bottom); stores along the Champs-Élysées (opposite top); Ladurée macarons (above); outside Brasserie Fouquet's (right).

Stroll the Champs-Élysées

AVENUE OF CHEERS

PARTY WITH THE PARADE

In 1789, things were tough for the people of France. Prices for food were high, and people had very little money. Meanwhile, the king and queen – and the nobles – were spending huge amounts of money. The people wanted a change. On 14 July 1789, they sacked a prison known as the Bastille (see pages 90-91) and began a long effort to overthrow the French monarchy and get back rights to the people. This marked the start of the French Revolution. Today, 14 July is known as **Bastille Day**. It is celebrated with parties, music, fireworks and parades. The Bastille Day parade is the oldest parade in Europe.

AU REVOIR

Fast Facts
Number of biking teams: **22**

Riders on each team: **8**

Year of the first Tour de France: **1903**

Prize money: **about US $2.5 million**

In 2024, on account of the Summer Olympics being held in Paris, the Tour de France finished in a different city for the first time in more than 100 years.

74 A Kid's Guide to PARIS

FANCY FIREWORKS
Bastille Day includes a dazzling fireworks show at the Eiffel Tower.

TOUR DE FRANCE

Want to catch a glimpse of the most challenging bicycle race in the entire world? Now's your chance! The **Tour de France** is a bicycle race that takes place each July. Unlike most races, though, this one lasts for nearly three weeks and stretches over 3,600 km (2,235 miles) – that's like cycling more than three times the length of France. Cyclists face steep mountain climbs, as well as flat stretches where they must cycle as quickly as they can; the rider with the fastest combined time from all the stages wins. The race's starting point changes from year to year, but it finishes down the Champs-Élysées.

IMAGES: Tour de France cyclists on the Champs-Élysées (left); a Bastille Day parade on the Champs-Élysées (opposite top); fireworks at the Eiffel Tower (above).

Stroll the Champs-Élysées

Arc de Triomphe

This iconic landmark, the **Arc de Triomphe**, was built to memorialise France's military victories. Here, at one end of the Champs-Élysées, 12 different roads from all directions meet, forming a sunlike plaza: the Place Charles de Gaulle.

In the early 1800s, Napoleon Bonaparte became the country's first emperor. He ordered the construction of the arch in 1806, and it was completed in 1836 – that's 30 years later! At the time, the Arc de Triomphe was the world's largest victory arch, reaching as high as a five-storey building. It's still one of the largest on the planet.

Visitors can take it all in and see the arch's intricate carvings up close. The monument is known for its sculptures, which show figures representing the French Revolution. Close to the arch, guests can also spot the **Tomb of the Unknown Soldier**, which honours French soldiers who have died.

IMAGE: Arc de Triomphe.

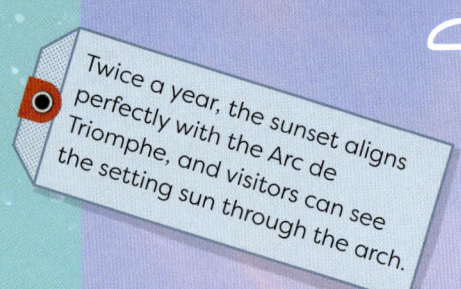

> Twice a year, the sunset aligns perfectly with the Arc de Triomphe, and visitors can see the setting sun through the arch.

ICONIC PARIS

Today, Paris is known for its grand, orderly avenues lined with trees and pristine buildings – but for much of its history, the city was a medieval jumble of stone and wood. That all changed in the 19th century, when an urban planner named Georges-Eugène Haussmann led a project, under the guidance of Napoleon III, to give the city a new look.

There are almost 300 steps leading to the top of the Arc de Triomphe! It's worth the climb to see stunning views of the city. (There is a lift, too!)

Stroll the Champs-Élysées 77

CATCH SOME CULTURE

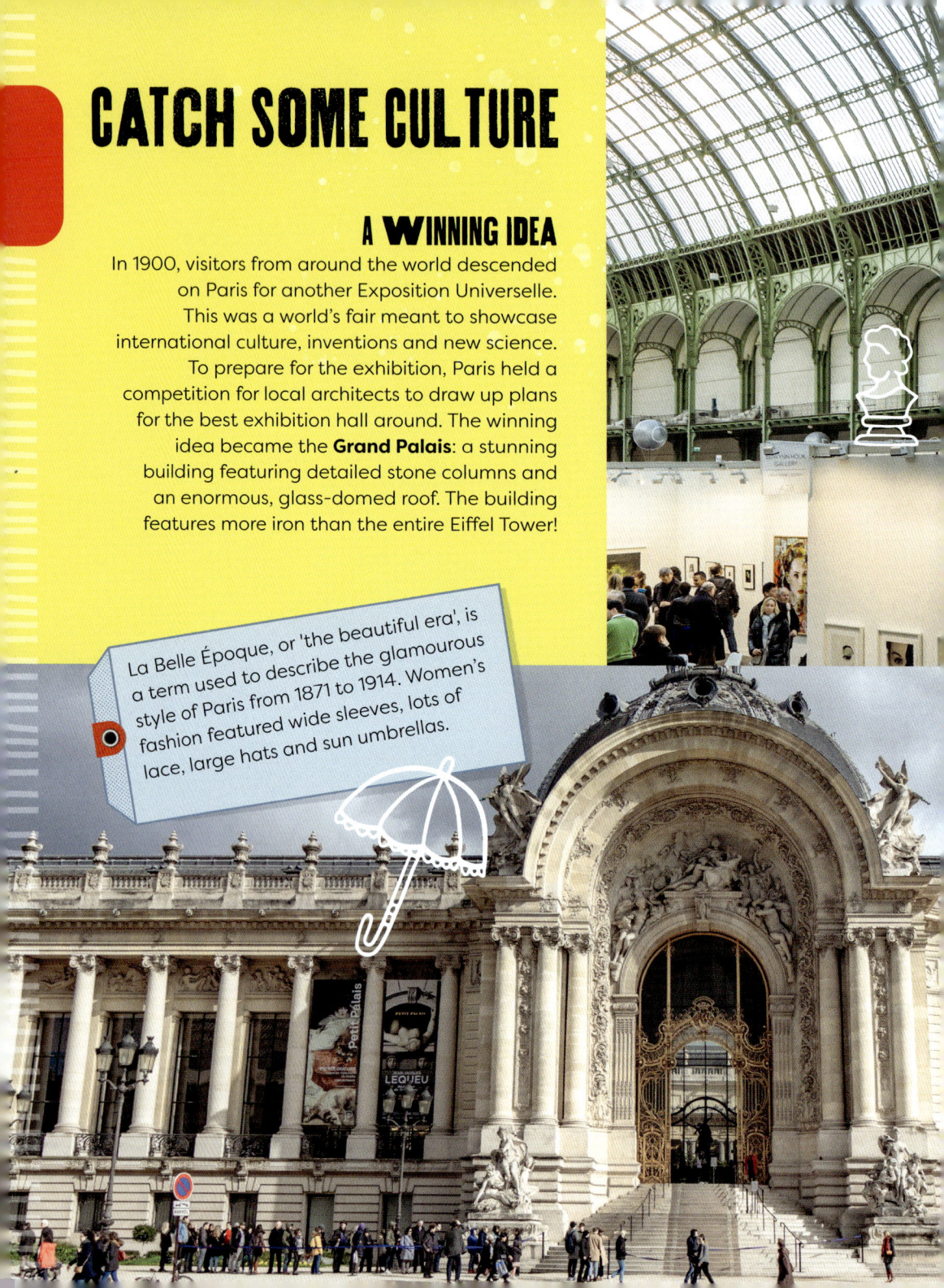

A WINNING IDEA

In 1900, visitors from around the world descended on Paris for another Exposition Universelle. This was a world's fair meant to showcase international culture, inventions and new science. To prepare for the exhibition, Paris held a competition for local architects to draw up plans for the best exhibition hall around. The winning idea became the **Grand Palais**: a stunning building featuring detailed stone columns and an enormous, glass-domed roof. The building features more iron than the entire Eiffel Tower!

La Belle Époque, or 'the beautiful era', is a term used to describe the glamourous style of Paris from 1871 to 1914. Women's fashion featured wide sleeves, lots of lace, large hats and sun umbrellas.

It took three years and 1,500 workers to build the Grand Palais.

PALACE OF THE ARTS

Despite its name, the **Petit Palais** was never a palace – unless you count it as a palace of art! Like its larger neighbour, the stunning structure was built in 1900 for the Exposition Universelle, and it became a museum in 1902. This museum of the arts is filled with golden statues, domed roofs and towering arches. Inside are masterpieces of painting and sculpture. Each gallery is 15 m (50 ft) long and painted with stories of Paris and the city's history. Here, you can also enjoy storytelling events, fun-filled workshops, or running around in the picturesque (and somewhat hidden!) courtyard.

IMAGES: Petit Palais (left); inside the Grand Palais (above).

Stroll the Champs-Élysées

A PLACE FOR PEACE

A SURPRISING HISTORY

Today, with its broad open spaces and stately buildings, the **Place de la Concorde**, a public square, seems rather peaceful. In fact, *concorde* means harmony. However, a gruesome history is hidden in these stones. During the French Revolution (see page 74), revolutionaries overturned the French monarchy and executed many of its ruling members. For several years, Place de la Concorde served as the site for many of these executions – in fact, it was at this spot that revolutionaries executed both King Louis XVI and Queen Marie-Antoinette.

FOUNTAINS AND FUN

Many visitors to the Place de la Concorde come to witness a historic site. However, many also come for the fountains! Bedecked in gold, the **Fontaine des Mers** (Fountain of Seas) and **Fontaine des Fleuves** (Fountain of Rivers) showcase bronze sculptures of ancient Roman water gods, mermaids and fish. Above them, stately jets of water arc and splash.

The Luxor Obelisk was originally part of a pair; the second remains at the Luxor Temple in Egypt.

FIT FOR A PHARAOH

At one end of the Place de la Concorde, you might notice an enormous obelisk, or pointed pillar, straight from ancient Egypt. This is the **Luxor Obelisk**, a granite pillar carved in Egypt more than 3,000 years ago! The monument was originally created to honour the ancient Egyptian pharaoh Ramses II. So, how did it end up here? The obelisk was given to France as a gift from Egypt and installed here in 1836.

IMAGES: Place de la Concorde (opposite); Fontaine des Fleuves (above); the base of Luxor Obelisk (left).

Stroll the Champs-Élysées

A MONUMENTAL CITY

A LA GLOIRE
DES GÉNÉRAUX
DE LA
RÉVOLUTION FRANÇAISE

VERSAILLES

Want to live like royalty for a day? Take a day trip to the **Château de Versailles** (Palace of Versailles), just 16 km (10 miles) outside of Paris. First constructed as a – very fancy – hunting lodge for King Louis XIII in 1624, it was transformed into the royal residences in 1661 under the next king, Louis XIV.

The palace is enormous! It sprawls across 63,154 sq m (679,784 sq ft) – that's the size of more than 240 tennis courts! There are countless windows, statues and decorations – the entire front gate is covered in gold leaf!

The grounds are sprawling, too. There are parks, gardens, horse stables, a canal and lake, a waterfall and more. Inside, things are just as grand. The 2,300 rooms hold many treasures – enormous paintings, marble statues and gold leaf as far as the eye can see. Visitors can peek at Queen Marie-Antoinette's chambers or stroll the Hall of Mirrors, a huge hallway full of enormous mirrors, glass chandeliers and lavishly painted ceilings.

IMAGES: Inside the Panthéon (previous page); Château de Versailles (right); Hall of Mirrors (opposite right).

BY THE NUMBERS

Versailles is a palace of epic proportions. Just look at the stats! The palace walls are dotted with 2,143 windows. Inside, 67 staircases offer an ascending path to the upper levels. And on top, over 1,200 chimneys poke out from the palace roof.

Marie-Antoinette, also a resident of Versailles, loved hot chocolate so much that she had her own personal chocolate maker on staff.

MORE PARISIAN PALACES

OPULENT SHOPS

Located just steps from the Louvre, **Palais-Royal** was built in the early 1600s and is now known for the *Colonnes de Buren*, 252 optical illusion-inducing black-and-white columns of varying sizes spread throughout the courtyard. As you explore, look down carefully – you'll see some columns extend underground into an almost-hidden pool!

PACK A LUNCH

Originally called Place Royale, this sightly square was once used as a practice area for duels – one-on-one battles! It's also the oldest square in France. It was first created as a place for nobles to escape the busy and then-messy streets of Paris. Today it's called **Place des Vosges**, a perfect place for a picnic among the picturesque buildings and grassy lawns. While here, visit the former home of Victor Hugo, famed author of the novel *Les Misérables*.

IMAGES: Place des Vosges (left); Palais-Royal courtyard (above); Palais du Luxembourg and its gardens (opposite top); gates of the Palais de l'Élysée (opposite bottom).

THE ROYAL TREATMENT

With its grand size and beautiful design, **Palais du Luxembourg** is a palace fit for a queen – and that's exactly what it was. Constructed for Queen Marie de Médicis in 1625, the building's Italian style reflected the queen's Italian heritage. Visitors can tour the gardens (see page 37) and the library, which holds 450,000 books!

During the French Revolution, Palais du Luxembourg was used as a prison.

PRESIDENTIAL PALACE

Palais de l'Élysée is a building steeped in history. First built in the early 1700s, the mansion was made for a French count. It became the home of the head of state in the late 1800s, and soon electricity and hot water was installed – very uncommon for the time. Today, it is the official residence of France's president. There are 365 rooms and 100 clocks inside. The grounds are covered with 100 species of trees and 12,000 flowers.

Macabre Monuments

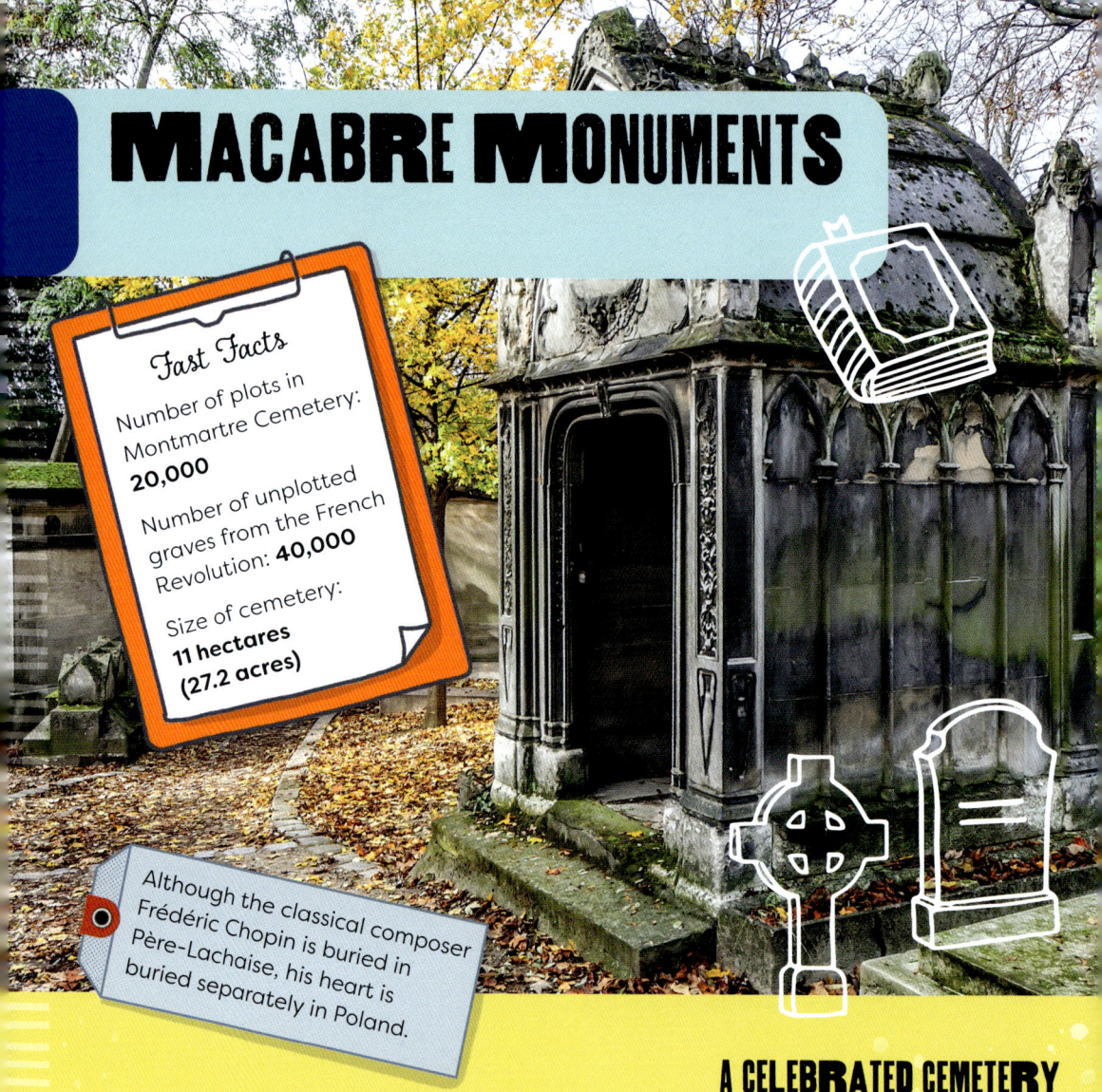

Fast Facts

Number of plots in Montmartre Cemetery: **20,000**

Number of unplotted graves from the French Revolution: **40,000**

Size of cemetery: **11 hectares (27.2 acres)**

Although the classical composer Frédéric Chopin is buried in Père-Lachaise, his heart is buried separately in Poland.

A Celebrated Cemetery

Paris is home to all kinds of monuments – including monuments to the dead. Often called the most visited cemetery in the world, **Père-Lachaise** is a sprawling graveyard of historic and famous tombs. Though the cemetery was established in 1804, the bones of some of its residents are much older than that. Originally built on the outskirts of Paris, the graveyard was considered to be too far out of town to draw much attention. To increase publicity and encourage people to bury their loved ones here, the administrators of Père-Lachaise had the remains of many famous people moved to the grounds. Today, this includes famous musicians (from Jim Morrison to Frédéric Chopin), famous writers (from Oscar Wilde to Gertrude Stein) and more.

SECRET CEMETERY

Though less well known than Père-Lachaise, **Cimetière de Montmartre** (Montmartre Cemetery) is definitely worth a visit. Opened in 1825, the graveyard is the resting place of many notable figures from French history, such as author Alexandre Dumas fils (son of Alexandre Dumas who wrote The Three Musketeers). It's the third largest cemetery in the city. Here, visitors can walk between the graves and tombs and look down from above as they cross the Rue Caulaincourt bridge.

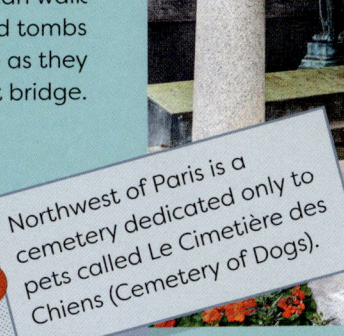

Northwest of Paris is a cemetery dedicated only to pets called Le Cimetière des Chiens (Cemetery of Dogs).

FOR THE PEOPLE

Located in Paris's Latin Quarter, the **Panthéon** looks like it would be more at home in ancient Rome thanks to its grand columns and domed roof. It was erected in the late 18th century and transformed into a monument for great French citizens after the French Revolution. Today, its crypt is the final resting place for many renowned French figures, such as author Victor Hugo and scientist Marie Curie. Curie was the first woman to rest here when she was moved to the Panthéon in 1995.

IMAGES: The Panthéon (left); a mausoleum at Père-Lachaise (opposite); the grave of Alexandre Dumas in Montmartre Cemetery (above).

A Monumental City 89

PEEK INTO THE PAST

MONUMENT TO THE PAST

Today, this historic site features a large, open square. However, more than 230 years ago, **Place de la Bastille** was the location of the Bastille, the most famous prison in Paris. Built as a fortress beginning in the 14th century, the Bastille was used as a jail under King Louis XIII in the 1600s. As times worsened for the people of France, the prison soon became a symbol of oppression (see page 74). On 14 July 1789, an angry mob stormed the Bastille, sparking what would become the French Revolution. The Bastille was eventually demolished – now, all that remains is this square.

STEP BACK IN TIME

Standing in the busy square surrounded by modern buildings and zooming cars, it may be tough to imagine what the Bastille might have looked like. Luckily, you don't have to! The **Timescope terminal** on the corner of Boulevard Richard Lenoir offers a 360-degree, 3D virtual reality view of what the site would have looked like in the past. Using a tall rotating machine with specialised binoculars, peer at the Bastille as it would have been in both 1416 and 1789!

ALWAYS IN STYLE

One of the oldest remaining streets in the city, **Rue du Faubourg Saint-Antoine** has been bustling since medieval times. In the 1400s, the street was known for its skilled cabinetmakers. There were 200 workshops in the area! Today, the stores are a bit more modern – but as popular as ever. While here, check out the maze of small passageways and courtyards around the street!

IMAGES: Place de la Bastille (opposite); an engraving of the Bastille (above); Rue du Faubourg Saint-Antoine (left).

A Monumental City 91

MASTERS OF ART

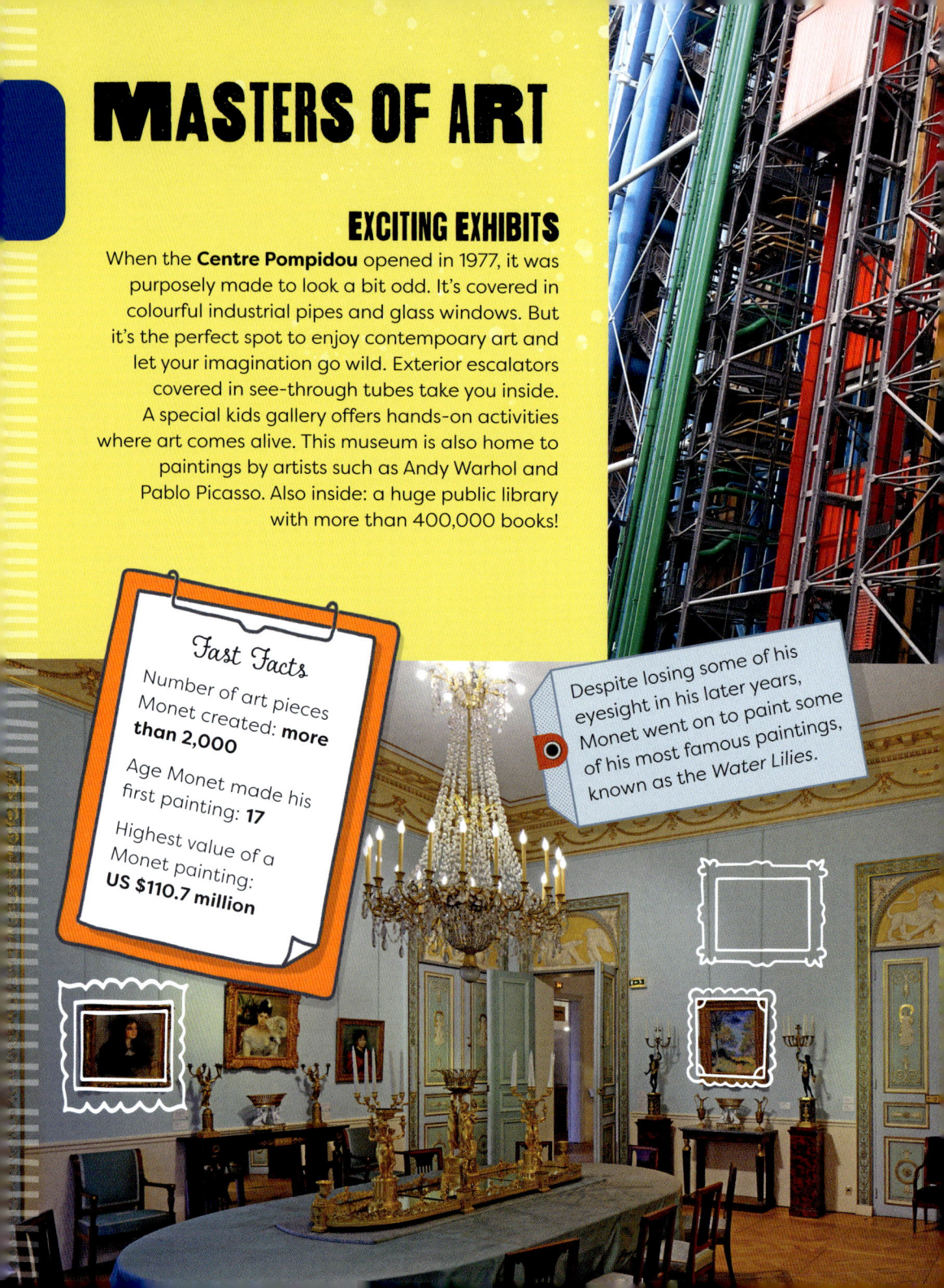

EXCITING EXHIBITS

When the **Centre Pompidou** opened in 1977, it was purposely made to look a bit odd. It's covered in colourful industrial pipes and glass windows. But it's the perfect spot to enjoy contempoary art and let your imagination go wild. Exterior escalators covered in see-through tubes take you inside. A special kids gallery offers hands-on activities where art comes alive. This museum is also home to paintings by artists such as Andy Warhol and Pablo Picasso. Also inside: a huge public library with more than 400,000 books!

Fast Facts

Number of art pieces Monet created: **more than 2,000**

Age Monet made his first painting: **17**

Highest value of a Monet painting: **US $110.7 million**

Despite losing some of his eyesight in his later years, Monet went on to paint some of his most famous paintings, known as the Water Lilies.

ANCIENT ART

Some of the oldest known art in the entire world is located in France. But it's not in a museum – it's in a cave! The Lascaux cave system in southwestern France contains paintings made by humans some 12,000 to 36,000 years ago.

MEET MONET

In 1790, a mansion known as the Château de la Muette was divided into smaller lots and sold. Nearly a century later, part of the property passed into the hands of an art lover named Jules Marmottan. Today, the **Musée Marmottan Monet** (Monet Museum) holds Marmottan's original collection of artistic masterpieces, as well as an enormous selection of works by the French Impressionist painter Claude Monet. In addition to the world's largest collection of works by Monet, the museum has pieces by Berthe Morisot, the first recognised female Impressionist painter, and other highlights, such as works from the Middle Ages.

IMAGES: Inside the Musée Marmottan Monet (left); Centre Pompidou (above).

A Monumental City

THE WILD SIDE

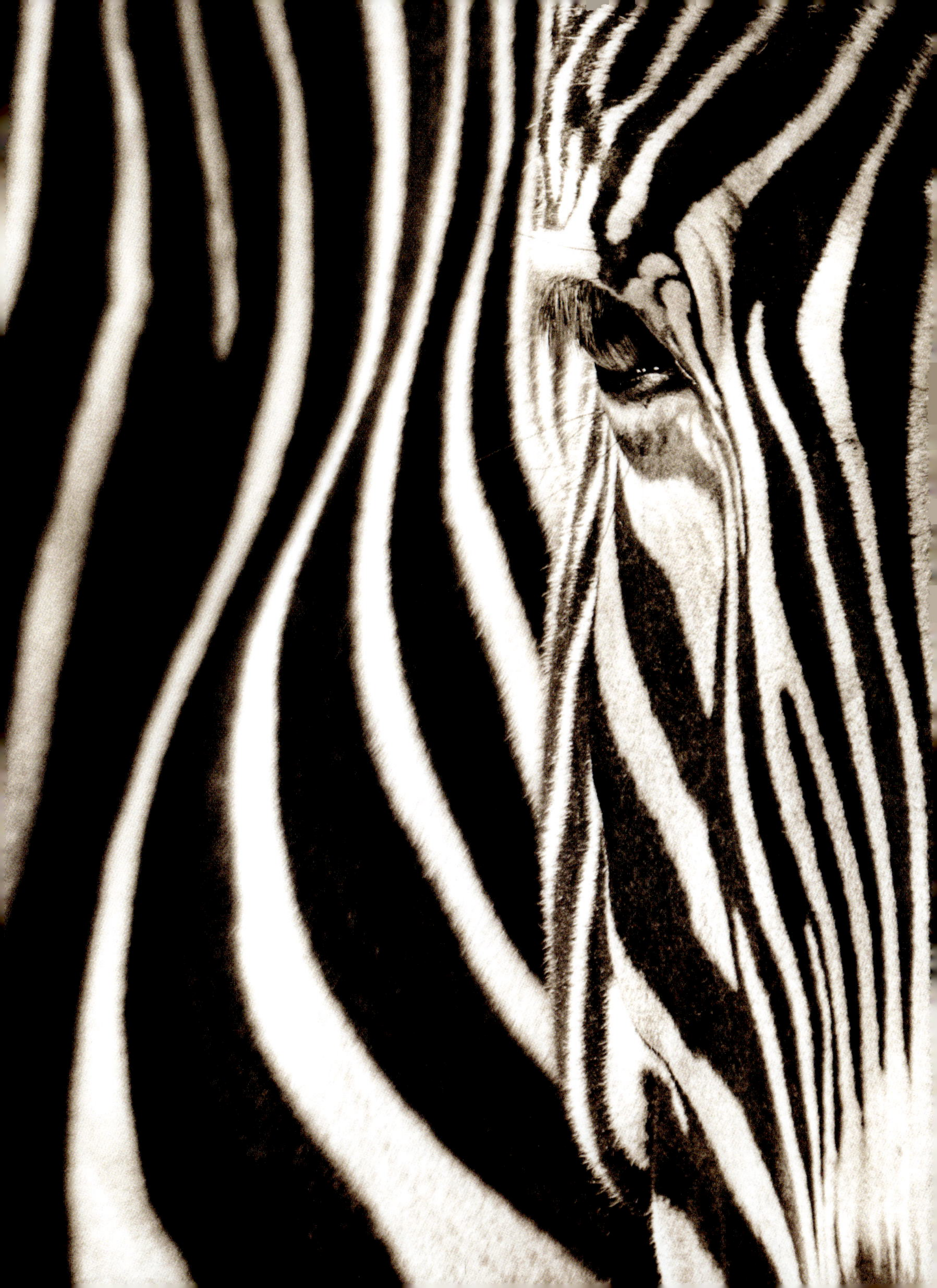

AMAZING ANIMALS

A WORLD OF WONDERS

A wild world exists within the bustling streets of Paris! Enter **Jardin des Plantes** to find sprawling gardens and greenhouses. Created as a medicinal garden for the king in 1635, the grounds contain more than 2,000 types of plants – and even some trees that are nearly 300 years old! What's more, the Jardin des Plantes is home to one of the world's oldest existing zoos. First opened in 1794, the Ménagerie now houses 1,200 animals. The zoo is also working to increase the populations of endangered animal species.

Fast Facts

Number of animal species: **about 255**

Zoo size: **14 hectares (34.5 acres); the size of 26 American football fields**

Highest point: **65 m (213 ft)**

GIRAFFE TRENDY
In the 1820s, the ruler of Egypt decided to send a gift to the king of France: a giraffe named Zarafa. She lived at the Ménagerie in the Jardin des Plantes – and was a French celebrity. In fact, Zarafa was so popular that many women even adopted a hairstyle based on the giraffe's horns.

At the Parc Zoologique de Paris, meet the bush dog – a small canid, or dog relative, that spends much of its time in the water.

ANIMAL KINGDOM

Ready to get wild? Head to the **Parc Zoologique de Paris** (Paris Zoological Park), an enormous zoo that contains some 3,000 animals! The zoo has five natural habitats so that visitors can observe the animals' true behaviours. Come face-to-face with incredible animals, such as lemurs, fossa, lions, rhinoceroses, sea lions, penguins and so much more. A focal point of the zoo is a gigantic 65-m (214-ft) mountain that has winding paths for wild sheep to walk along! The zoo also has special programmes dedicated to saving endangered animals, such as the Antillean manatee and the Chilean puma.

IMAGES: A zebra at Parc Zoologique de Paris (previous page); a manatee at Parc Zoologique de Paris (left); Jardin des Plantes (above).

The Wild Side 97

MAKE A SPLASH

COOL CANALS

Come on in, the water's fine! Enjoy swimming at the **Bassin de la Villette**, where human-made outdoor pools let you swim safely in a Parisian canal basin. You'll also find lots of water sport activities and equipment, pedal boats, kayaks and more. If swimming isn't your scene, head to **Canal Saint-Martin**, a trendy neighbourhood situated on a stunning canal that flows into the basin. Stroll or bicycle by the historic canal, which was first created in 1825, or see the sights from the water on a cool canal cruise. Make sure to pop into the local bakeries for a pick-me-up snack!

IMAGES: Bassin de la Villette (above); Paris Plages on the Seine (opposite top); waterslides at Aquaboulevard de Paris (opposite bottom).

HIT THE BEACH

Paris is far from the coast – but that doesn't mean it lacks a beach. During the **Paris Plages** summer event, the city creates artificial beaches along the Seine and at Bassin de la Villette. You'll find plenty of beach chairs, umbrellas and even palm trees! The beaches along Bassin de la Villette even have showers and changing huts. What's more – there are local vendors on hand selling snacks and ice cream.

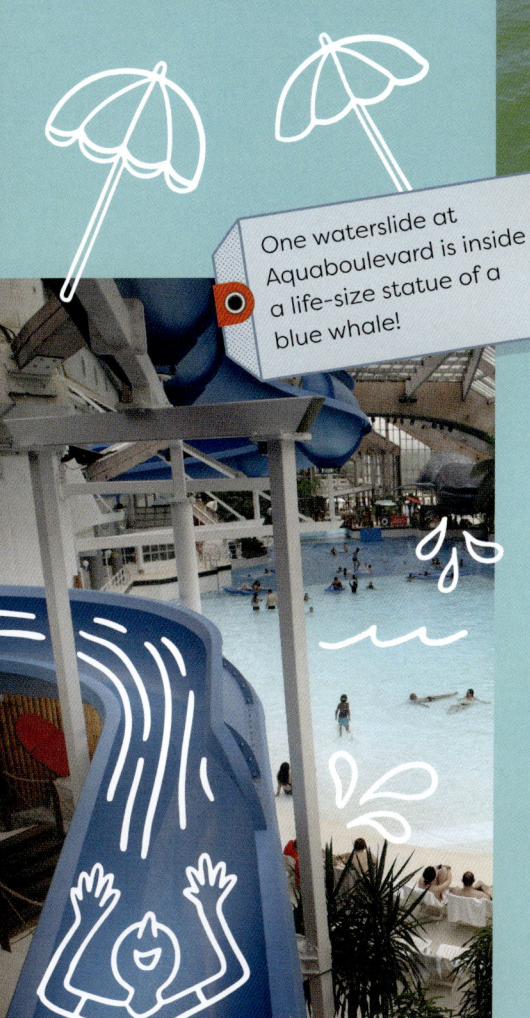

One waterslide at Aquaboulevard is inside a life-size statue of a blue whale!

Fast Facts

Aquaboulevard park size: **7,000 sq m (75,000 sq ft)** – about the size of five Olympic swimming pools

Number of waterslides: **11**

POOL PARTY

Get ready to hit the water at **Aquaboulevard de Paris**! This enormous water park is the largest urban water park in all of France. Zip down the waterslides, splash in the wave pools, float down lazy rivers, warm up in the hot tubs and more. You can even relax at a sandy beach that stretches more than 3 km (2 miles) long.

The Wild Side 99

Hike Up High

Paris might be a bustling urban centre, but that doesn't mean you can't stretch your legs and go for a nice hike. Grab your gear and head for the hills of **Montmartre**, a historic Parisian neighbourhood.

There are several ways to reach the top – including taking the funicular (see pages 30-31) – but the most fun way might be to climb the steps to **Basilique du Sacré-Coeur** (Sacred Heart Basilica), built in the late 1800s and early 1900s and famed for its many white domes.

You'll need to hike up nearly 300 stairs – so pack a reusable water bottle! – but the views are more than worth it. If you're looking for an even more challenging activity, you can climb to the top of Sacré-Coeur's central dome, too!

Nearby, be sure to check out some of the other sites of Montmartre. Close to Sacré-Coeur is one of the oldest churches in Paris, **Paroisse Saint-Pierre de Montmartre**. Pop into nearby shops to pick up souvenirs. Look around for seasonal food carts – if you're around in winter, be sure to sample the roasted chestnuts!

> Sacré-Coeur stays blindingly white thanks to its limestone blocks: when it rains, the stones secrete a white substance that then hardens.

IMAGES: Basilique du Sacré-Coeur (right); outside the Moulin Rouge (opposite).

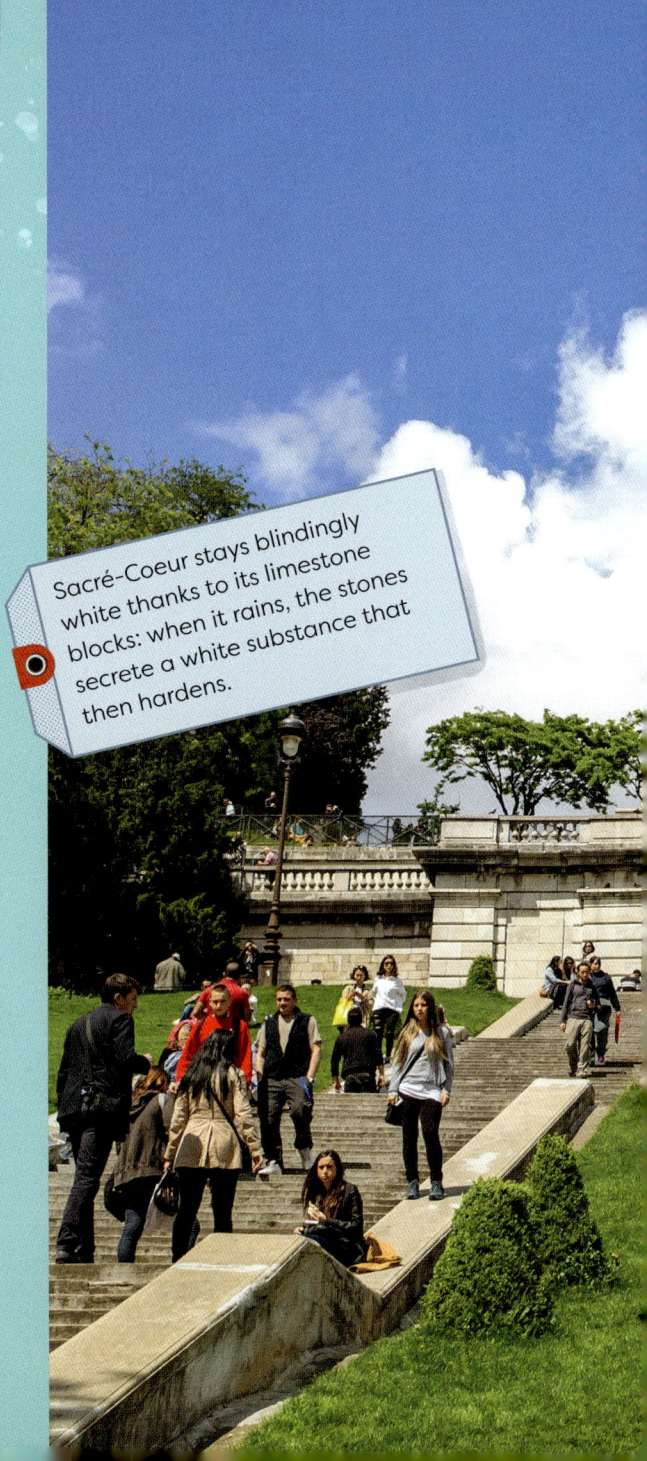

Fast Facts

Years of construction: **from 1875 to 1923**

Central dome height: **83 m (272 ft)**

Width: **35 m (115 ft)**

Length: **83 m (272 ft)**

YES, WE CANCAN!

One of the most famous cabaret theatres in the world, the Moulin Rouge in Pigalle (at the foot of Montmartre) is known for the red windmill on its roof ('moulin rouge' means 'red mill' in French). Originally, the venue was founded as a dance hall, where its performers created a new style of dancing that showcased high kicks and was known as the cancan.

The Wild Side 101

WILD INDOORS

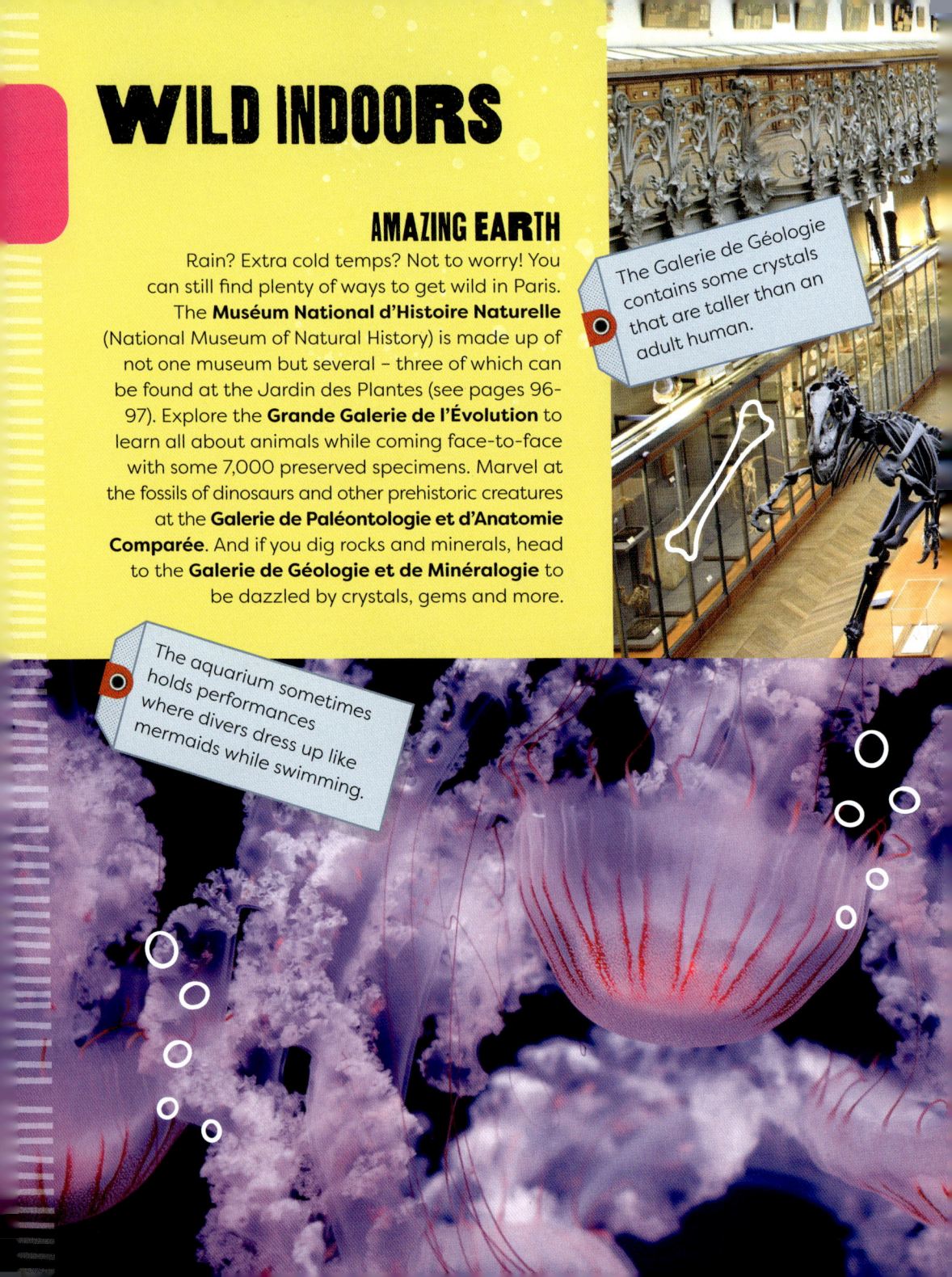

AMAZING EARTH

Rain? Extra cold temps? Not to worry! You can still find plenty of ways to get wild in Paris. The **Muséum National d'Histoire Naturelle** (National Museum of Natural History) is made up of not one museum but several – three of which can be found at the Jardin des Plantes (see pages 96-97). Explore the **Grande Galerie de l'Évolution** to learn all about animals while coming face-to-face with some 7,000 preserved specimens. Marvel at the fossils of dinosaurs and other prehistoric creatures at the **Galerie de Paléontologie et d'Anatomie Comparée**. And if you dig rocks and minerals, head to the **Galerie de Géologie et de Minéralogie** to be dazzled by crystals, gems and more.

The Galerie de Géologie contains some crystals that are taller than an adult human.

The aquarium sometimes holds performances where divers dress up like mermaids while swimming.

A TINY TERROR

One type of dinosaur that lived in the area that is now France was *Compsognathus*. About the size of a modern-day chicken, this tiny dino lived 150 million years ago. It was likely very swift and used its speed to chase down even smaller prey.

WATERY WONDERS

Dive into the **Aquarium de Paris** to explore the wonders of the ocean. First founded in 1867, this aquarium was one of the first in existence. Home to 13,000 sea animals, the aquarium is dedicated to supporting ocean conservation. Check out the massive shark tank and its more than 38 large sharks! Be mesmerised by the 2,500 jellies at the Médusarium, the largest jelly tank in Europe, or explore the 700 colourful coral colonies.

Fast Facts

Species of sharks in aquarium: **4**

Species of jellies in aquarium: **more than 55**

Amount of food the animals eat each month: **0.9 tonnes (1 ton)**

IMAGES: Jellies at the Aquarium de Paris (left); fossils at Muséum National d'Histoire Naturelle (opposite top); Compsognathus (above).

The Wild Side 103

BE AN URBAN EXPLORER

LOOP THE LATIN QUARTER

One of the oldest areas of Paris, the **Latin Quarter** is where the ancient Romans set up camp. Here among the neighbourhood's winding cobblestone streets you'll find historic buildings and ruins, including the ancient Roman amphitheatre known as the **Arènes de Lutèce** that used to seat 15,000 people!

MEANDER LE MARAIS

The area of **Le Marais** was originally a swamp. Today it's known for its modern trendiness and charm and features narrow streets and 17th century mansions. Discover lots of quirky shops, picnic in the parks, or explore the **Jewish Quarter** to find bountiful bakeries for a delicious bite. You can also explore sites created by the Knights Templar, a renowned medieval group of crusader soldiers.

STROLL SAINT-GERMAIN

Saint-Germain (or Saint-Germain-des-Prés, as it is officially called) is a charming historic district in the heart of Paris. With its postcard-perfect cafés, like **Les Deux Magots**, and pastry shops full of French treats, this neighbourhood seems straight out of a movie. It is also home to the oldest chocolate shop in all of Paris. The **À la Mère de Famille** opened in 1761 – it's more than 260 years old!

BE WELCOME IN BELLEVILLE

Get off the beaten path in **Belleville**. This lively neighbourhood is the perfect place to explore various outdoor and indoor food and flea markets. Belleville is also a place where many international cultures meet. Sample some Algerian or Chinese food, or take it to go and head to **Parc de Belleville**. At 128 m (420 ft) above sea level, it's the perfect spot to take in the picturesque Paris skyline.

IMAGES: The Latin Quarter at night (opposite top); Les Deux Magots in Saint-Germain (above); shopping in Belleville (right); cafés in Le Marais (opposite bottom).

GOING GREEN

IMAGE: Parc des Buttes-Chaumont.

REPURPOSED PARKS

PARISIAN WILDLIFE
Looking to spot wildlife around the city? Keep your eyes peeled for lots of birds – including common species, such as pigeons and sparrows, plus rarer appearances by Eurasian kestrels, geese and ducks – as well as red foxes, red squirrels and more.

TOP OF THE LINE!
Paris has many stunning parks, but the **Promenade Plantée** is head and shoulders above the rest – literally! At some 10 m (33 ft) above the ground, the beautiful green space is located on a viaduct, or elevated bridge, that used to hold train tracks. Now the former tracks have been transformed into a lush green walkway with trees, flowers and even pools.

A PECULIAR PAST

Today, **Parc des Buttes-Chaumont** is a stunning site, featuring a quiet lake, green cliffs and even a waterfall flowing inside a hidden grotto. But centuries ago, the region was not quite so pleasant. In medieval times it was where prisoners were executed. At one point it was also a quarry – a place where people mined for minerals – and a dumping ground for sewage! Luckily, the quarry was cleaned up in the 19th century and turned into the pretty park it is today.

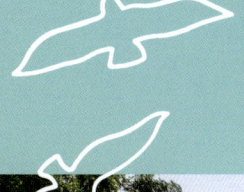

TRAIL ON THE TRACKS

Before the creation of the Paris metro (see pages 24-25), people needed a way to get around the city. Luckily for them they had the **Petite Ceinture**, or 'little belt', a railway that circled Paris. But after being abandoned in 1934, the train tracks became overgrown. Now the tracks host more than 200 species of animals and plants. Several parts have officially been turned into walkways and parks, making for lovely – and somewhat secret! – green spots throughout the city.

IMAGES: Eurasian kestrel (opposite bottom); roses at the Promenade Plantée (opposite top); Parc des Buttes-Chaumont (above); Petite Ceinture (left).

Going Green

GARDENS GALORE

FIT FOR A QUEEN

The gardens of Paris are some of the finest in the world – and it's no surprise when you consider that many were built for royalty! In the late 16th century, Queen Catherine de' Medici ordered the creation of **Jardin des Tuileries**, or Tuileries Garden. Here, ride an old-fashioned carousel or take in the view from the top of the Jeu de Paume. And don't miss the statue of Puss in Boots at the foot of a statue of Charles Perrault, the French author who created the character. Visitors can also sail toy boats in the Grand Bassin pond, play on the playgrounds and even jump on giant trampolines!

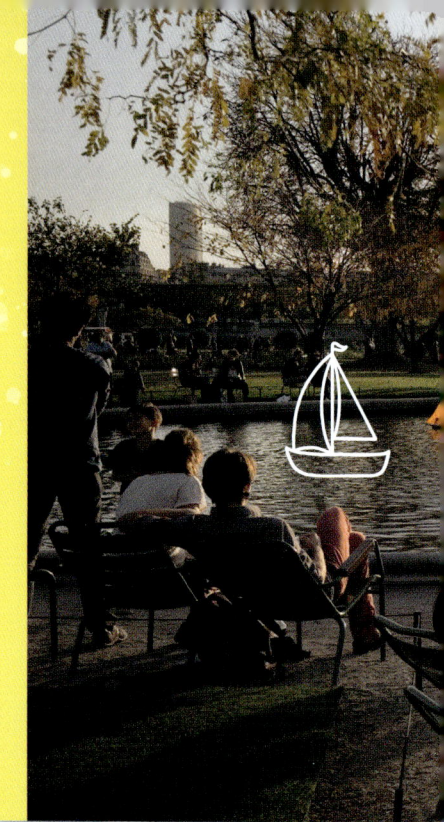

GREEN WITH ENVY

Paris boasts some of the most interesting botanical gardens in the world! The Botanical Garden of the Pharmaceutical and Biological Sciences College showcases some 400 species of medicinal – and poisonous – plants!

King Louis XIII once had his own private zoo located in Tuileries Garden.

TAKE A TRIP

Travel to far-flung parts of the world without ever leaving Paris by entering the **Jardin des Serres d'Auteuil**, inside Bois de Boulogne, a public park. First created in 1761, this garden features more than 15,000 species of tropical plants. The plants are housed in five historic greenhouses dating from the 19th century. Discover brightly coloured orchids, towering palms and tempting papaya trees. Get up close to cacti and other desert wonders or stroll through the Japanese gardens. You can even stop by carp ponds or aviaries full of colourful birds.

IMAGES: Jardin des Serres d'Auteuil (left); Jardin des Tuileries (above).

Going Green

ISLAND SIGHTS

If you're looking for the true heart of Paris, look no further than **Île de la Cité**, an island in the middle of the Seine. Some 2,300 years ago, a Celtic tribe settled here, marking the beginnings of what would become Paris.

Today, the island is a peaceful getaway and a hub of history. Start your journey by crossing the oldest bridge in Paris: Pont Neuf, first built in 1578. Make your way to the **Square du Vert-Galant**, a somewhat secret park perfect for picnics. Then head to **Sainte-Chapelle**, a Gothic-style chapel built inside a medieval royal palace where kings of France once lived. Nearby, another can't-miss spot is the **Conciergerie**. Originally a medieval palace, the site was transformed into a prison in the 14th century. It later housed Queen Marie-Antoinette.

Keep walking to make your way to the iconic Notre-Dame Cathedral (see page 50). And be sure to look for Point Zero, a bronze plaque in front of the cathedral marking the very centre of Paris!

IMAGE: Pont Neuf and Île de la Cité.

Nine different bridges connect two islands to the mainland of Paris.

ISLAND HOPPING

Nearby the Île de la Cité is a smaller, even quieter island: the Île Saint-Louis. Head here to gawk at centuries-old buildings, including one of Paris's oldest hotels, or stop for ice cream! The Berthillon ice creamery has been around since 1954. It quickly became famous for its ultra-creamy treat made from a secret recipe.

Art, Naturally!

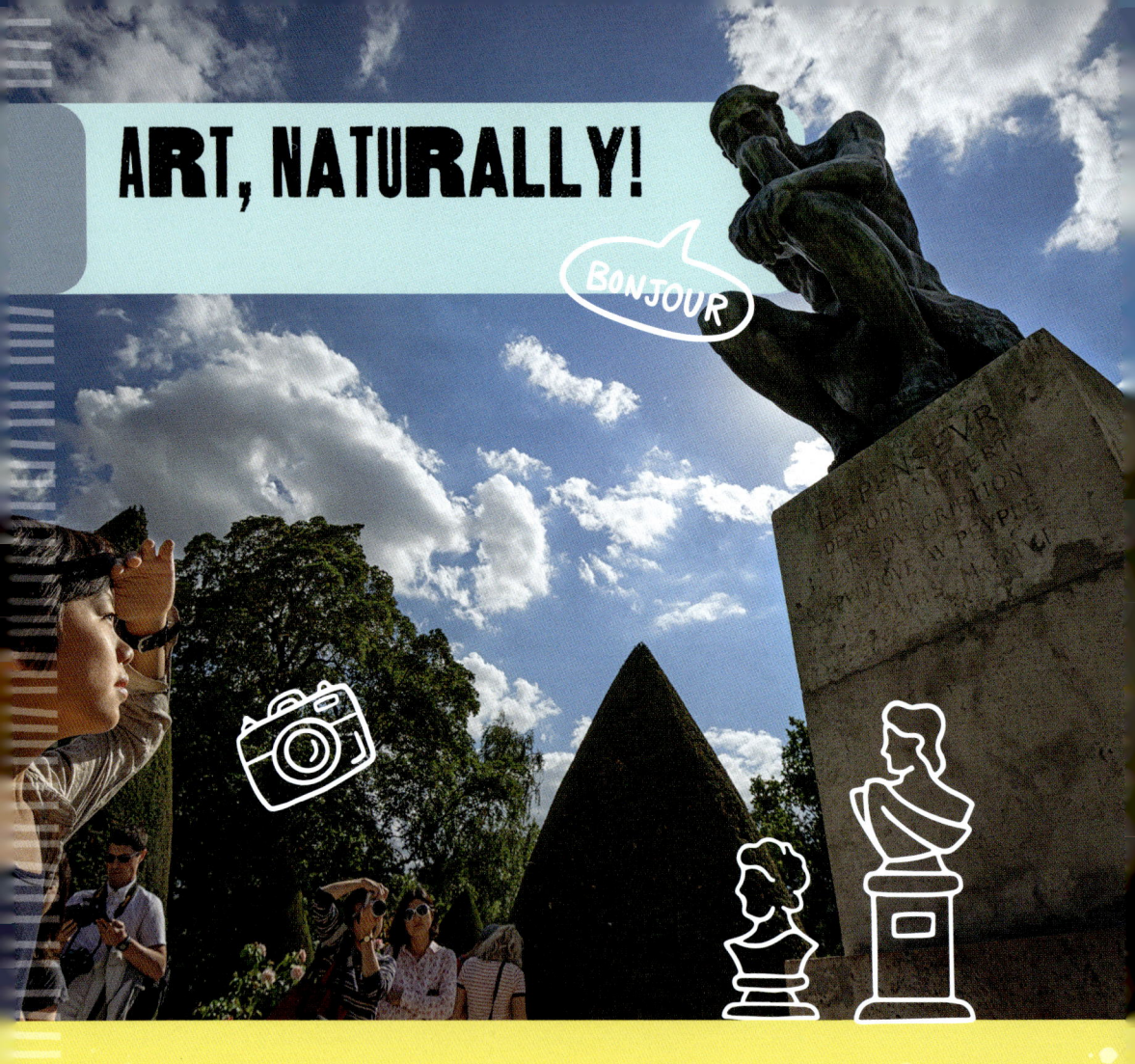

Bonjour

Think on It

What could be better than taking in the natural beauty of the great outdoors? Immersing yourself in some art, too! At the **Musée Rodin** (Rodin Museum), guests can view works of art by the great French sculptor Auguste Rodin, who was responsible for famed pieces such as *The Thinker*. Best of all is the sculpture garden, where visitors can view Rodin's works amid the changing seasons. Set against a backdrop of changing leaves or blooming flowers, the statues seem to come alive.

IMAGES: The Thinker at Musée Rodin (above); Donald Duck mosaic street art by Invader (opposite top); Stravinsky Fountain (opposite bottom).

IT'S AN INVASION!

Did you know that Paris is home to lots of outdoor art as well? From murals to graffiti, gorgeous street art lines the city's walkways and sides of buildings. You can spot this art wherever you go – as long as you keep your eyes peeled! One of the most famous French street artists is an anonymous artist known as Invader. Invader is known for mosaics of space aliens and more, which can be found throughout Paris – as well as in 78 other cities around the world!

> The French street artist Invader has created art pieces that can only be discovered by scuba divers.

Fast Facts
Number of Invader mosaics around the world: **over 4,000**

Number of continents with Invader art: **6**

Height of highest space invader: **2,362 m (7,750 ft)**

SPITTING IMAGES

This next destination takes the phrase 'soaking up some art' to a whole new level! Located in the Beaubourg neighbourhood, the **Stravinsky Fountain** includes 16 wildly coloured art sculptures, some of which spit water. Created by artists Jean Tinguely and Niki de Saint Phalle, the fun fountain sculptures were inspired by the music of famous composer Igor Stravinsky. There is even a QR code visitors can scan to listen to a soundtrack meant to accompany the dancing fountains.

Going Green 115

LOVELY LAKES

GO WILD

Want to get away from it all? Head to **Lac Inférieur** inside Bois de Boulogne, a bit of wilderness that offers a breath of fresh air in the bustling city. Perfect for bird-watching, the lake is also home to a small island that can be reached by boat. The area even includes a campground where you can spend the night. It feels miles away, but you're still in Paris!

IMAGES: Canoes on Lac Inférieur (above); sailboats at Île de Loisirs de Saint-Quentin-en-Yvelines (opposite top); Île de Loisirs de Bois-le-Roi (opposite bottom).

116   A Kid's Guide to PARIS

FUN IN THE SUN

If you're looking to make a real splash and get a bit more active, consider making the short trip to **Île de Loisirs de Saint-Quentin-en-Yvelines**. It's located about 25 km (15.5 miles) outside of Paris and has plenty of kayaking, sailing, mini golf and more. There's even a farm! In the wild, don't forget to keep your eyes open to spot deer, eagles and beavers.

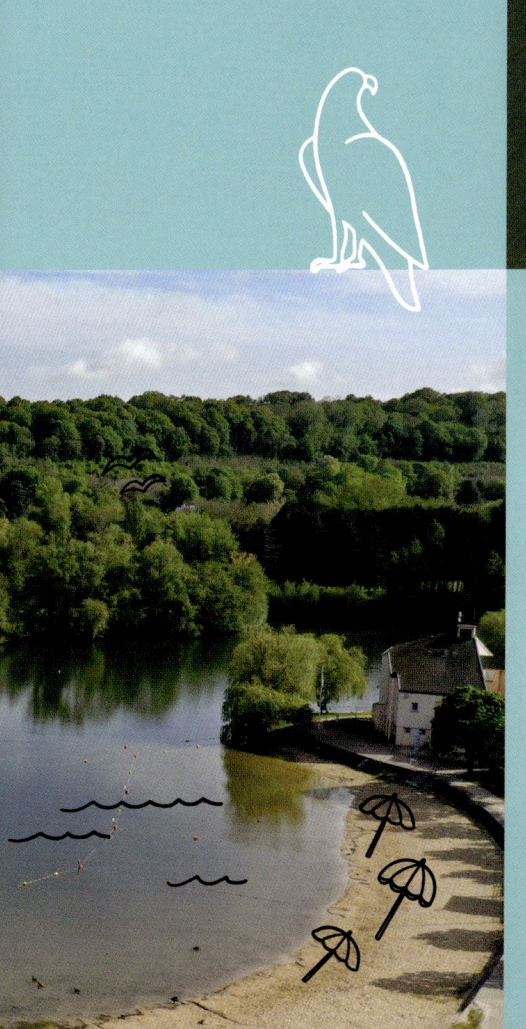

BEACH BOUND

Surf's up at the **Île de Loisirs de Bois-le-Roi**! If you're willing to take a short day trip, this lake is ranked as one of the best places to swim near Paris. At just 50 km (31 miles) outside of the city, the lake is well worth the drive. On top of sandy beaches, here you can hit the splash pad, shoot some hoops, play beach volleyball, go mountain biking and try some rock climbing.

Going Green 117

SECRETS OF THE CITY

IMAGE: The Paris Catacombs.

GO UNDERGROUND

> To get into the catacombs, visitors must walk down 131 steps – and then up 112 to get out!

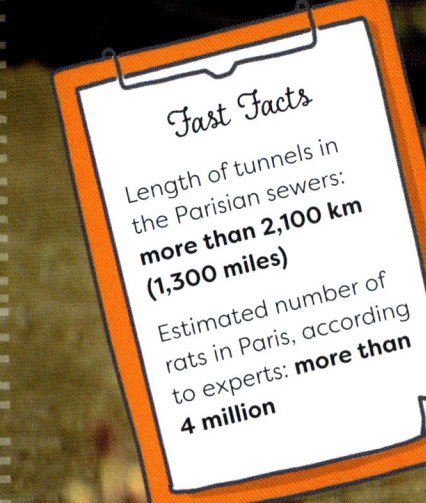

NO BONES ABOUT IT

Get ready to explore a secret city that stretches far beneath the streets of Paris – a city of the dead, that is! Some 20 m (65 ft) below the city surface, the **Catacombes de Paris** (Catacombs of Paris) are home to the centuries-old skeletal remains of millions of people. Ancient Romans first created these tunnels around 2,000 years ago when they were mining for stone. But it wasn't until the late 18th century, when Paris's cemeteries became overcrowded, that the tunnels were filled with skeletons. Today, visitors can explore a 1.6-km-long (1 mile) long loop to view these historic bones, many of which have been purposefully arranged in artistic patterns.

Fast Facts

Length of tunnels in the Parisian sewers: **more than 2,100 km (1,300 miles)**

Estimated number of rats in Paris, according to experts: **more than 4 million**

EERIE EVENTS

For the past several centuries, people have hosted special – and sometimes secret – events in the catacombs. These have included movie screenings, orchestras, parties and fancy dinners.

STINKY SURROUNDINGS

Ah, Paris – city of love, lights, and . . . sewers? That's right: though it lies hidden underground, the Parisian sewer system is essential for keeping the streets free from waste and disease. At the **Musée des Égouts de Paris** (Museum of Sewers), visitors can experience the secrets of the sewers firsthand. Learn about the importance of the sewers, from their historic, funky beginnings to citywide cleanup efforts. Discover the amazing engineering required to build and maintain the system and the different jobs required to keep the city clean. And – if you can stomach the smell – you can even tour working sewer tunnels to see the magic for yourself.

IMAGES: Stacked bones in the Catacombs of Paris (above); a sewer rat (left).

Secrets of the City 121

BUSTLING MARKETS

If you're looking to explore Paris like a local, consider setting off on a tour of the city's markets. Held on various days of the week, these indoor and outdoor marketplaces (called *marchés*) are teeming with delicious food, fantastic sights and even hidden treasures!

One of the oldest markets in Paris, **Marché aux Fleurs Reine Elizabeth II** on the Île de la Cité, has been bursting with colourful flowers each Sunday since 1830. If you're feeling peckish, head instead to **Marché Beauvau**. There, you'll find vendors selling delicious local cheeses, baguettes and more.

But the most exciting of all the markets might be **Marché aux Puces de Saint-Ouen**: a sprawling collection of mysterious antiques, rare books and more wonderful trinkets. Divided into 14 mini markets, it has more than 2,000 vendors selling all sorts of delights. Whatever you like, you will probably find it here!

Marché aux Puces de Saint-Ouen is the largest antique market in the entire world.

IMAGES: Marché aux Puces de Saint-Ouen (right); Futuro House (opposite).

122 A Kid's Guide to PARIS

SEE A SPACESHIP
Pop into Marché Dauphine, one of the many marketplaces within Marché aux Puces de Saint-Ouen, for a surprising sight: a giant orange spaceship! This alien-esque structure is actually a futuristic-style house designed in 1968 as part of a series. These 'Futuro Houses' were never actually lived in. Now they are collector's items.

SEARCH FOR UNICORNS

A set of tapestries like the ones at Musée de Cluny might have taken a team of 30 or so weavers more than 18 months to complete.

A MEDIEVAL MANSION

The impressive Hôtel des Abbés de Cluny was built in 1485 and resembles a Gothic castle. The former fancy residence is now the **Musée de Cluny** (Cluny Museum), a museum dedicated to medieval artefacts. Here, there's a collection of six tapestries woven sometime around the year 1500. Known as *The Lady and the Unicorn*, the tapestries feature a young woman and a mysterious unicorn. What's more, the museum even has a real unicorn horn! Of course, experts today know that the horn did not truly belong to a unicorn. But in medieval times, the 'unicorn horn' was thought to be a powerful and magical item.

A room built of feathers, a 'unicorn' horn and taxidermied animals can also be found at the unusual Musée de la Chasse et de la Nature, the Museum of Hunting and Nature.

A Kid's Guide to PARIS

STRANGE COLLECTIONS

For more weird museums, check out the Musée d'Histoire de la Médecine, or the Museum of the History of Medicine. The museum showcases historic – and sometimes frightening – medical equipment and traces the progress of surgery through the ages.

CABINET OF CURIOSITIES

Part museum, part shop, **Deyrolle** is an emporium of oddities. Founded in 1831 by French naturalist Émile Deyrolle, the shop features a wide, rotating collection of animal taxidermy, rare gems, preserved insects and more. Here, you can admire strange works of art featuring elements from the natural world. Perhaps the most incredible of Deyrolle's collections are its unicorns – taxidermied horses made to look like the mythical creatures . . . or even a pegasus!

IMAGES: Taxidermy at Deyrolle (left); unicorn tapestry at Musée de Cluny (above).

Secrets of the City

SECRET STOPS

TAKING TEA
Exploring a new city can be exhausting – why not take a well-deserved break at the **Grande Mosquée de Paris**? This stunning mosque, which was built in the 1920s, contains a beautiful and relaxing courtyard and gardens. Guests can also visit certain prayer rooms with fine carpets or enjoy a snack while sipping mint tea in the restaurant. The mosque features a 33-m (108-ft) minaret – a thin tower at the top of the mosque.

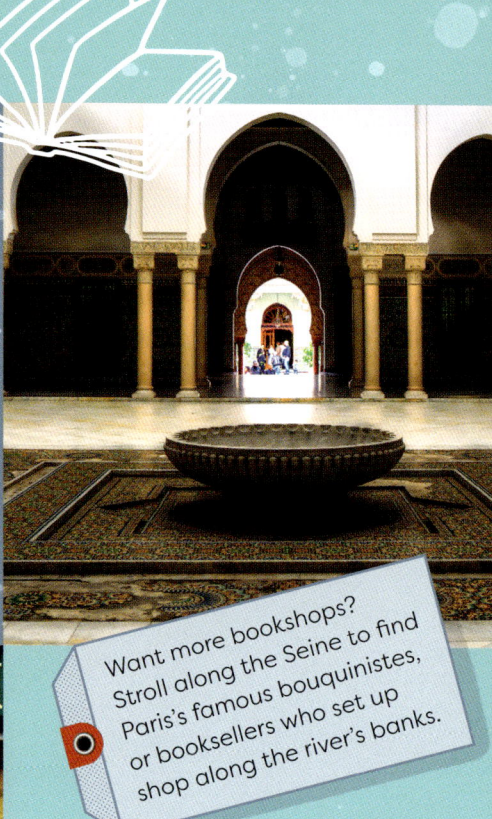

Want more bookshops? Stroll along the Seine to find Paris's famous bouquinistes, or booksellers who set up shop along the river's banks.

TURN THE PAGE
Calling all bookworms: **Shakespeare and Company** is one of the most famous bookshops on the planet! First opened in 1951, this winding shop was a favourite stop of many famous writers throughout the decades. Today, it is easy to get lost in the rows of used, new and rare books. Take your time – books are tucked into every nook and cranny!

NEW YORK, NEW YORK!

Have a hankering for a glimpse of the Statue of Liberty? Don't worry – you don't need to go all the way to New York! A replica of the statue (about a quarter of the size of the original) sits on a small island, named **Île aux Cygnes**, in the middle of the Seine. The statue was gifted to France in 1889 by American citizens in honour of the anniversary of the French Revolution (see page 74).

IMAGES: The courtyard of the Grande Mosquée de Paris (opposite top); Paris's miniature Statue of Liberty (left); frogs legs cooked in butter with garlic, parsley and lemon (bottom); reading at Shakespeare and Company (opposite bottom).

HOP TO IT

Though it may seem unusual to some foreigners who are not used to the dish, frog legs are a popular meal in France. If you'd like to give the dish a try, there's nowhere better than **Roger La Grenouille**, a historic frog-themed restaurant. First opened in 1930, the restaurant was enjoyed by popular artist Pablo Picasso and even Queen Elizabeth II of England.

Secrets of the City 127

CITY OF LOVE

LOVE YOU LOCKS

Spanning the Seine, the historic **Pont des Arts** is an iconic site in Paris. It was a romantic one, too: over the decades, strolling couples paid tribute to their love by attaching 'love locks' to the bridge. These locks were padlocks decorated with the couples' initials or other messages. The practice has since been banned – the weight of the locks was causing damage to the bridge! – but the spot remains a symbol of love.

IMAGES: Love locks formerly on the Pont des Arts (above); Mur des Je t'aime (opposite top); Le Coeur de Paris (opposite bottom).

128 A Kid's Guide to PARIS

SWEET SAYINGS

Search out a prime photo opportunity at the **Mur des Je t'aime**, or *I Love You Wall*, a large mural that says 'I love you' in 250 languages. The mural, which is located in Montmartre and spans 39 sq m (416 sq ft), was created by two artists as a monument to the universality of love.

The artist behind the Mur des Je t'aime collected many translations simply by walking around Paris and having people write down 'I love you' in their native language.

WE HEART PARIS

Want to show your adoration for Paris? Come view **Le Coeur de Paris**, an enormous art installation of a giant heart located in Porte de Clignancourt. Created in 2019, the sculpture is covered in 3,800 hand-painted tiles. It also rotates and even lights up in a heartbeat rhythm!

Speaking of hearts – Paris is the final resting place for the heart of the famous French philosopher Voltaire; it has been preserved in a heart-shaped casket inside the Bibliothèque Nationale de Paris (National Library).

Secrets of the City 129

WHAT'S THE DIFFERENCE?

Paris is known for its beauty – with a city that looks like this, it makes perfect sense! Can you spot the five differences between these two pictures? See answers on page 140.

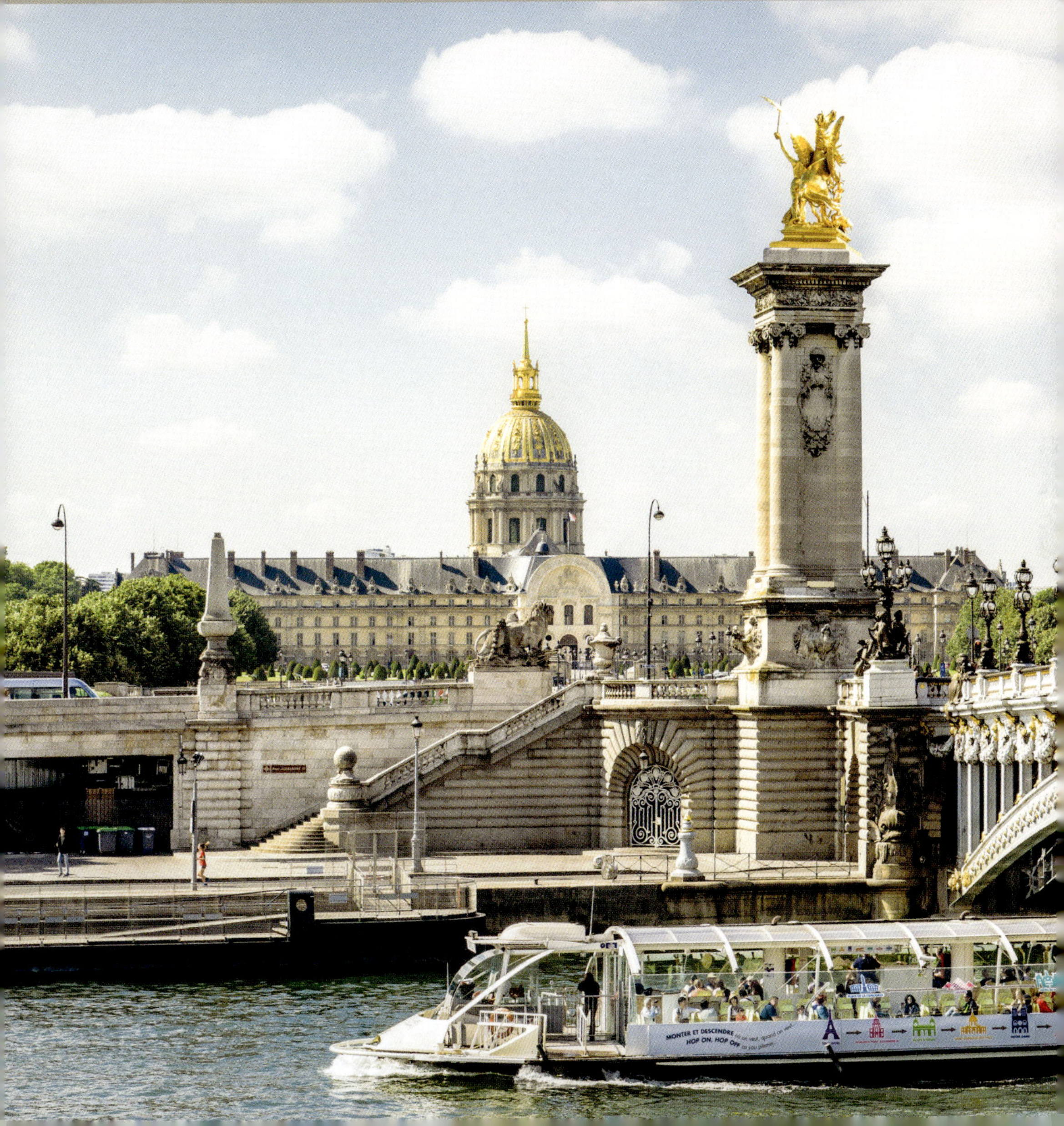
MONTER ET DESCENDRE
HOP ON, HOP OFF as you please

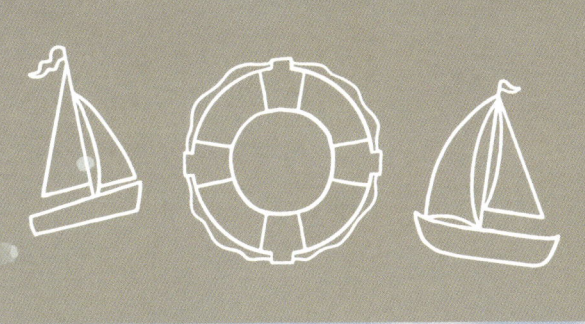

WHAT'S THE DIFFERENCE?

Overlooking the heart of Paris, Sacré-Coeur is one of the city's most iconic monuments. Can you spot the five differences between these two pictures? See answers on page 140.

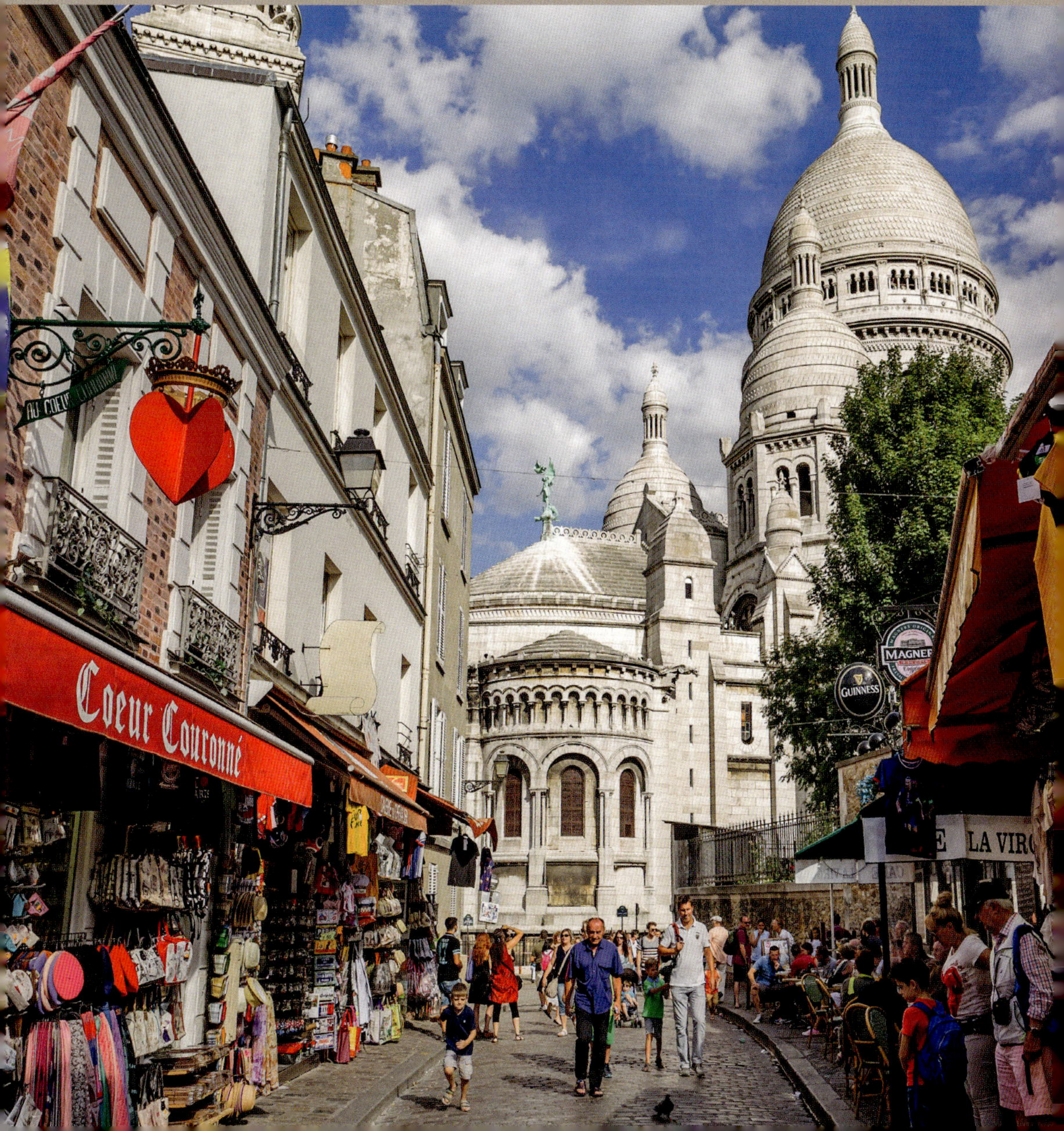
Coeur Couronné
MAGNERS
GUINNESS

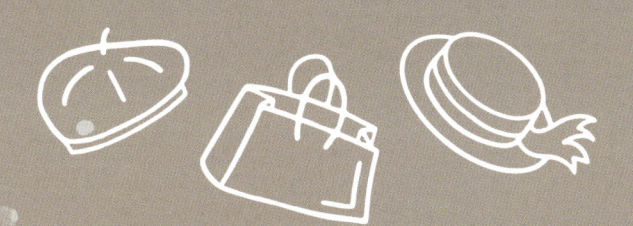

INDEX

A
À la Mère de Famille chocolate shop 105
amusement parks
    Aquaboulevard de Paris 99, **99**
    Disneyland Paris 29, 38-39, **38-39**
    Jardin d'Acclimatation 37, **37**
    Musée des Arts Forains 35, **35**
    Parc Astérix **32-33**, 38-39, **38-39**
Aquaboulevard de Paris 99, **99**
Aquarium de Paris 102-103, **102-103**
Arc de Triomphe **15**, **23**, **70-71**, 76-77, **76-77**
art museums. See museums
Arts et Métiers metro station 24
Atelier des Lumières 34, **34**

B
baguettes 58, **58**
bánh mì sandwich 69, **69**
Ballon de Paris Generali 48, **48-49**
Basilique du Sacrè-Coeur 100-101,
    100-101, **132-133**, **140**
Bassin de la Villette 98, **98**, **99**
Bastille 74, 90, 91, **91**
Bastille Day 74-75, **74-75**
Batobus **20-21**, 21
beaches 99, **99**, 117, **117**
La Belle Époque 78
Belleville 105, **105**
Berthillon ice creamery 112
Bibliothèque Nationale 129
bistro foods 63
Bois de Boulogne **110-111**, 111, 116, **116**
bookshops 126, **126**
Brasserie Fouquet's 73, **73**
breakdancing 42
Brie cheese 59, **59**
buses 22, **22**, 23

C
cable car (funicular) 30-31, **30-31**, 100
cabs 22, **22**
Canal Saint-Martin 98
catacombs 12, **15**, **118-119**, 120-121, **120-121**
Cathédrale Notre-Dame de Paris 12, **15**,
    50-51, **50-51**, **141**
Catherine de' Medici, Queen 110
cemeteries 88-89, **88-89**. See also catacombs
Centre Pompidou 92, **92-93**
Champs-Élysées 70-81
    Arc de Triomphe **15**, **23**, **70-71**, 76-77, **76-77**
    Bastille Day 74-75, **74-75**
    Grand Palais 78-79, **78-79**
    luxury shopping and dining 72-73, **72-73**
    Petit Palais **78-79**, 79
    Place de la Concorde **15**, **80-81**, **80-81**
    Tour de France 74-75, **74-75**
Charles VI, King 59
Château de Versailles 29, 84-85, **84-85**
Châtelet-Les Halles metro station 24
cheese 59, **59**, 60, 61
Chopin, Frédéric 88
churches
    Notre-Dame 12, **15**, **50**, 50-51, **51**, **141**
    Paroisse Saint-Pierre de Montmartre 100
    Sacré-Coeur 100-101, **100-101**, **132-133**, **140**
    Saint Gervais **26-27**
Cité des Sciences et de l'Industrie **15**, 35, **35**, 36
Le Coeur de Paris 129, **129**
concert halls and theatres 40-41, **40-41**, 101, **101**
Conciergerie 112
crêpes 61, **61**
croissants **56-57**, 58, **58**
Cronut 68
croque madame sandwich 61, **61**
croque monsieur sandwich 61, **61**
Curie, Marie 89
cycling 26, **26-27**, 27, 74-75, **74-75**

D
da Vinci, Leonardo 52, 53
Les Deux Magots 105, **105**
Deyrolle, Émile 125
Disneyland Paris 29, 38-39, **38-39**
Dumas, Alexandre 89, **89**

E
éclairs 64, **64**
Eiffel, Gustave 47
Eiffel Tower
    about 46-47, **46-47**
    Bastille Day fireworks 75
    on map 15
    night lights 13, **13**
    from Pont Alexandre III **12-13**
    at sunset **44-45**
Elizabeth II, Queen of England 127
escargots (snails) 66-67, **66-67**
Exposition Universelle (world's fair) 26, 46, 78, 79

F
falafel 68, **68**

Favand, Jean Paul 35
Fontaine des Fleuves 81, **81**
Fontaine des Mers 81
food 56-69
    Berthillon ice creamery 112
    bistro foods 63
    bread and cheese **56-57,** 58-59,**58-59,** 60, 61
    Champs-Élysées 73, **73**
    escargots (snails) 66-67, **66-67**
    French fries **61,** 63, **63**
    French onion soup 62, **62-63**
    frog legs 127, **127**
    global grub 68-69, **68-69**
    lunch 60-61, **60-61**
    ratatouille 62, **62-63**
    Saint-Germain 105, **105**
    sweets 64-65, **64-65,** 73, **73**
fountains 81, **81,** 115, **115**
French fries **61,** 63, **63**
French onion soup 62, **62-63**
French phrases 10
French Revolution 74, 80, 87, 88, 90
frites (French fries) **61,** 63, **63**
frog legs 127, **127**
funicular 30-31, **30-31,** 100
Futuro House 123, **123**

G
gardens. *See* parks and gardens
Generali Balloon of Paris 48, **48-49**
golf cart tours 23, **23**
Grand Palais 78-79, **78-79**
Grande Mosquée de Paris 126, **126**
Grévin Museum 34, **34**
Guerlain perfumery 72, **72**

H
Haussmann, Georges-Eugène 76
hot-air balloons 48-49, **48-49**
Hugo, Victor 86, 89

I
I Love You Wall 129, **129**
Île aux Cygnes 127, **127**
Île de la Cité 112-113, **112-113,** 122.
See also Notre-Dame Cathedral
Île de Loisirs de Bois-le-Roi 117, **117**
Île de Loisirs de Saint-Quentin-en-Yvelines 117, **117**
Île Saint-Louis 112, 113
Impressionist art 55, **92-93,** 93
Invader (street artist) 115

J
jambon-beurre sandwich 60, **60**
Jardin d'Acclimatation 37, **37**
Jardin des Plantes 96-97, **96-97**

Jardin des Serres d'Auteuil **110-111,** 111
Jardin des Tuileries **23,** 110, **110-111**
Jardin du Luxembourg 37, **37**
Jardins du Trocadéro 46
Jewish Quarter 104

L
Ladurée pastry house 73, **73**
lakes 116-117, **116-117**
Lascaux cave 93
Latin Quarter 104, **104**
Le Coeur de Paris 129, **129**
Le Marais 104, **104**
Leroux, Gaston 41
lights 13, **13,** 34, **34**
Louis XIII, King 84, 90, 110
Louis XIV, King **34,** 66, 84
Louis XVI, King 80
Louvre **15,** 52-53, **52-53**
'love locks' 128, **128**
Luxor Obelisk **80,** 81, **81**

M
macarons 73, **73**
maps 14-15, 17
Le Marais 104, **104**
Marché aux Fleurs Reine Elizabeth II 122
Marché aux Puces de Saint-Ouen 122-123, **122-123**
Marché Beauvau 122
Marie-Antoinette, Queen 80, 84, 85, 112
Marie de Médicis, Queen 72, 87
markets 122-123, **122-123**
Marmottan, Jules 93
metro 16, **16,** 17, **18-19,** 24-25, **24-25**
mille-feuille pastry 65, **65**
Mona Lisa (Leonardo da Vinci) 12, 52, 53, **53**
Monet, Claude 92-93
Montmartre
    Cimetière de Montmartre 88, 89, **89**
    funicular 30-31, **30-31,** 100
    hiking 100
    Mur des Je t'aime 129, **129**
    Paroisse Saint-Pierre de Montmartre 100
    Sacré-Coeur 100-101, **100-101, 132-133, 140**
    Square Louise Michel **8-9**
Montparnasse Tower **48-49,** 49
Morisot, Berthe 93
Morrison, Jim 88
mosque 126, **126**
Moulin Rouge 101, **101**
museums
    Atelier des Lumières (lights) 34, **34**
    Centre Pompidou (contemporary art) 92, **92-93**
    Cité des Sciences et de l'Industrie (science) **15,** 35, **35,** 36
    Crypte Archéologique (Roman ruins) 51, **51**
    Deyrolle (oddities) **124-125,** 125

Index **135**

Musée de Cluny (medieval artifacts) 124, **124–125**
Musée de la Chasse et de la Nature
  (hunting and nature) 124
Musée de Louvre (art) 12, **15**, 52–53, **52–53**
Musée des Arts Forains (fair rides) 35, **35**
Musée des Égouts de Paris (sewers) 121
Musée d'Histoire de la Médecine
  (history of medicine) 125
Musée d'Orsay (Impressionist art) **15**, 54–55,
  54–55
Musée Grévin (wax statues) 34, **34**
Musée Marmottan Monet
  (Impressionist art) **92–93**, 93
Muséum National d'Histoire Naturelle
  (natural history) 102–103, **102–103**
Musée Rodin (sculptures) 114, **114**
Petit Palais (art) **78–79**, 79
Mur des Je t'aime 129, **129**
musicians 25, **25**, 88

N

Napoleon Bonaparte, Emperor 76
Napoleon III, Emperor 72, 76
National Museum of Natural History 102–103,
  102–103
Noctilien (night bus) 23
Notre-Dame Cathedral 12, **15**, 50–51, **50–51**, 141

O

Olympics 42, 74
Opéra cake 65, **65**
opera house 40–41, **40–41**

P

Palace of Versailles 29, 84–85, **84–85**
Palais de l'Élysée 87, **87**
Palais du Luxembourg 37, **37**, 87, **87**
Palais Garnier 40–41, **40–41**
Palais-Royal 86, **86**
Panthéon **82–83**, 89, **89**
Parc Astérix **32–33**, 38–39, **38–39**
Parc Zoologique de Paris **94–95**, 96–97, **96–97**
Paris-Brest pastry 64, **64**
Paris Plages 99, **99**
parkour 43, **43**
parks and gardens. *See also* amusement parks
  Jardin d'Acclimatation 37, **37**
  Jardin des Plantes 96–97, **96–97**
  Jardin des Serres d'Auteuil **110–111**, 111
  Jardin des Tuileries 23, 110, **110–111**
  Jardin du Dragon 36, **36**
  Jardin du Luxembourg 37, **37**
  Jardins du Trocadéro 46
  medicinal plants 110
  Parc de Belleville 105
  Parc de la Villette 36, **36**

Parc des Buttes-Chaumont **106–107**, 109, **109**
Petite Ceinture 109, **109**
Place des Vosges 86, **86**
Promenade Plantée 108, **108**
Square du Vert-Galant 112
Square Louise Michel **8–9**
Paroisse Saint-Pierre de Montmartre 100
pastries 64–65, **64–65**
Pei, I. M. 52
Père-Lachaise cemetery 88, **88**
perfume 72, **72**
Perrault, Charles 110
pet cemetery 89
Petit Palais **78–79**, 79
Petite Ceinture 109, **109**
The Phantom of the Opera (Leroux) 41
Philharmonie de Paris 41, **41**
Picasso, Pablo 92, 127
Place Charles de Gaulle 76
Place de la Bastille 90, **90**
Place de la Concorde **15**, 80–81, **80–81**
Place des Vosges 86, **86**
playgrounds 36, **36**
Point Zero 112
Pont des Arts 128, **128**
Pont Neuf **20–21**, 112, **112–113**
pools 98, **98**
presidential palace 87, **87**
Promenade Plantée 108, **108**

R

ratatouille 62, **62–63**
RER (Réseau Express Régional train) 29, **29**
Rive Droite 14
Rive Gauche 14
Robert, Alain 49
Rodin, Auguste 114
Roger La Grenouille restaurant 127
roller coasters **32–33**, 38–39, **38–39**
Roquefort cheese 59, **59**
Rue du Faubourg Saint-Antoine 91, **91**

S

Sainte-Chapelle 112
Sacré-Coeur 100–101, **100–101**, **132–133**, 140
Saint-Germain 105, **105**
Saint Gervais Church **26–27**
Saint Phalle, Niki de 115
Seine River
  beach 99, **99**
  biking **26–27**
  boat rides 12, 20–21, **20–21**, 141
  Eiffel Tower 46, **46–47**
  goddess 141
  on map 14
  Pont des Arts 128, **128**

136 A Kid's Guide to PARIS

Pont Neuf **20-21**, 112, **112-113**
sewers 120-121, **120-121**
Shakespeare and Company bookshop 126, **126**
shopping
    Belleville 105, **105**
    bookshops 126, **126**
    Champs-Élysées 72-73, **72-73**
    markets 122-123, **122-123**
shows and concerts 40-41, **40-41**, 101, **101**
snails (escargots) 66-67, **66-67**
sports
    Olympics 42, 74
    parkour 43, **43**
    Stade de France 42, **42-43**
    swimming and water sports 98-99, **98-99**, 116-117, **116-117**
Square du Vert-Galant 112
Square Louise Michel, Montmartre **8-9**
St Honoré pastry 65
Stade de France 42, **42-43**
Statue of Liberty 37, 127, **127**
steak frites 63
Stein, Gertrude 88
Stravinsky Fountain 115, **115**
Stravinsky, Igor 115
street art 115, **115**
subway (metro) 16, **16**, 17, **18-19**, 24-25, **24-25**
Summer Olympics (2024) 42, 74
swimming and water sports 98-99, **98-99**, 116-117, **116-117**

T
tagine 69, **69**
taxis 22, **22**
theatres 40-41, **40-41**, 101, **101**
Timescope terminal 91
Tinguely, Jean 115
Tomb of the Unknown Soldier 76
trains 28-29, **28-29**
trams (trolleys) 28, **28-29**
Transilien (train) 29, **29**
Tuileries Garden **23**, 110, **110-111**

U
unicorns, in museums 124, **124-125**, 125

V
vegetarian quiche 63
Versailles 29, 84-85, **84-85**
Voltaire 129

W
walking 26, **26-27**
Warhol, Andy 92
water sports 98-99, **98-99**, 116-117, **116-117**

waterpark 99, **99**
What's the Difference? **130-133**, **140**
Wilde, Oscar 88
wildlife 108, **108**, 116, 117. *See also* zoos and aquariums
world's fair 26, 46, 78, 79

Z
zoos and aquariums
    Aquarium de Paris 102-103, **102-103**
    Jardin des Plantes 96-97
    Louis XIII's 110
    Parc Zoologique de Paris **94-95**, 96-97, **96-97**

Index 137

RESOURCES & PHOTO CREDITS

Getting Around Town (pages 18-31)
Batobus: batobus.com
Paris Metro: metromap.fr
RATP: ratp.fr
Transilien: transilien.com
Vélib': velib-metropole.fr

Places to Play (pages 32-43)
Atelier des Lumières: atelier-lumieres.com
Cité des Sciences et de l'Industrie: cite-sciences.fr
Disneyland Paris: disneylandparis.com
Jardin d'Acclimatation: jardindacclimatation.fr
Musée des Arts Forains: arts-forains.com
Musée Grévin: grevin-paris.com
Opéra National de Paris: operadeparis.fr
Parc Astérix: parcasterix.fr
Philharmonie de Paris: philharmoniedeparis.fr
Stade de France: www.stadefrance.com

What a View! (pages 44-55)
Ballon de Paris Generali: ballondeparis.com
Cathédrale Notre-Dame: notredamedeparis.fr
Crypte Archéologique: crypte.paris.fr
Eiffel Tower: toureiffel.paris
Montparnasse Tower: tourmontparnasse56.com
Musée de Louvre: collections.louvre.fr
Musée d'Orsay: musee-orsay.fr

Let's Eat! (pages 56-69)
L'Escargot Montorgueil: escargotmontorgueil.com

Stroll the Champs-Élysées (pages 70-81)
Arc de Triomphe: paris-arc-de-triomphe.fr
Grand Palais: grandpalais.fr
Ladurée: maisonladuree.com
Petit Palais: petitpalais.paris.fr
Tour de France: letour.fr

A Monumental City (pages 82-93)
Centre Pompidou: centrepompidou.fr
Château de Versailles: chateauversailles.fr
Musée Marmottan Monet: marmottan.fr
Palais de l'Élysée: elysee.fr/en/cultural-space/evreux-300
Palais du Luxembourg: senat.fr/lng/en/the-luxembourg-palace.html
Panthéon: paris-pantheon.fr

The Wild Side (pages 94-105)
Aquaboulevard de Paris: aquaboulevard.fr
Aquarium de Paris: aquariumdeparis.co
Basilique du Sacré-Coeur: sacre-coeur-montmartre.com m
Canal Saint-Martin: canauxrama.com
Jardin des Plantes: jardindesplantesdeparis.fr
Muséum National d'Histoire Naturelle: mnhn.fr
Parc Zoologique de Paris: parczoologiquedeparis.fr

Going Green (pages 106-117)
Conciergerie: paris-conciergerie.fr
Jardin des Tuileries: louvre.fr/en/explore/the-gardens
Musée Rodin: musee-rodin.fr

Secrets of the City (pages 118-129)
Catacombes de Paris: catacombes.paris.fr
Deyrolle: deyrolle.com
Grande Mosquée de Paris: grandemosqueedeparis.fr
Musée de Cluny: musee-moyenage.fr
Musée des Égouts de Paris: musee-egouts.paris.fr
Shakespeare and Company: shakespeareandcompany.com

138 A Kid's Guide to PARIS

IMAGE CREDITS
Illustration © 2025 Carolyn Sewell
8-9: Pierre Ogeron/Getty Images / **12-13:** Delpixart/Getty Images (cyclists); Neirfy/Shutterstock (Night Bridge) / **14-15:** Peter Hermes Furian (map); Alexander Spatari/Getty Images (Arc de Triomphe); Pigprox/Shutterstock (Louvre); Jan-Otto/Getty Images (Eiffel Tower); Anna Linda Knoll/Shutterstock (Citeé des Sciences et de l'industrie); Gwengoat/Getty Images (Musée d'Orsay); Viacheslav Lopatin/Shutterstock (Catacombs); Buena Vista Images/Getty Images (Place de la Concorde); Ed Spratt/EyeEm/Getty Images (Notre-Dame) / **16:** Maremagnum/Getty Images (metro station) / **17:** Fabrice LEROUGE/Getty Images / **18-19:** GOER/Shutterstock / **20-21:** Evannovostro/Shutterstock (Batobus); Romain Villa Photographe/Getty Images (Seine River) / **22:** Jasmina007/Getty Images (person with map); Pawel Libera/Getty Images (taxi) / **23:** Henry St John/Shutterstock (golf cart); Ioan Panaite/Shutterstock (car traffic) / **24-25:** Dmitry Brizhatyuk/Shutterstock (metro sign); Steve Lovegrove/Shutterstock (musicians) / **26-27:** Charday Penn/Getty Images (person with bicycle); olrat/Getty Images (walking by restaurant) / **28-29:** Leonid Andronov/Getty Images (tram); Benson Truong/Shutterstock (train); Kirill Neiezhmakov/Shutterstock (RER) / **30-31:** Delpixart/Getty Images / **32-33:** Henri0711/Shutterstock / **34:** Yuri Turkov/Shutterstock (wax figure); Pack-Shot/Shutterstock (digital art) / **35:** Matt Munro/Lonely Planet (carousel); Tommy Larey/Shutterstock (science museum) / **36:** Peeradontax/Shutterstock (folly); Tommy Larey/Shutterstock (slide) / **37:** AlexKozlov/Getty Images (gardens); Elena Dijour/Shutterstock (carousel) / **38-39:** Ferreiro/Shutterstock (Disneyland); page frederique/Shutterstock (Parc Astérix) / **40-41:** Christian Mueller/Shutterstock (Philharmonie); Songquan Deng/Shutterstock (Palais Garnier) / **42-43:** Yuri Turkov/Shutterstock (Stade de France); Vagengeim/Shutterstock (parkour) / **44-45:** © Frédéric Collin/Getty Images / **46-47:** espiegle/Getty Images (Eiffel Tower); Imgorthand/Getty Images (taking photo) / **48-49:** kavalenkau/Shutterstock (observation deck); DaylightLoren/Getty Images (balloon) / **50:** neirfy/Getty Images / **51:** Page Light Studios/Shutterstock (crypt); Víctor Augusto Mendívil/Getty Images (grotesque) / **52-53:** Pigprox/Shutterstock (Louvre); S-F/Shutterstock (*Mona Lisa*) / **54:** Stephen Bridger/Shutterstock (people with painting); ikmerc/Shutterstock (clock) / **55:** sokolovski/Shutterstock (museum interior); Gwengoat/Getty Images (museum exterior) / **56-57:** Artens/Shutterstock / **58:** Pietro Karras/Stocksy (croissant); Alexander Spatari/Getty Images (baguettes) / **59:** lechatnoir/Getty Images (Brie); istetiana/Getty Images (Roquefort) / **60:** ALLEKO/Getty Images / **61:** Petr Jilek/Shutterstock (crêpe); Kirstin Mckee/Stocksy (sandwiches) / **62-63:** Olives for Dinner/Getty Images (ratatouille); GMVozd/Getty Images (French onion soup); PM20/Shutterstock (fries) / **64:** serts/Getty Images (éclairs); Black Lollipop/Getty Images (Paris-Brests) / **65:** Liliia Bielopolska/Shutterstock (Opéra cake); Visionsi/Shutterstock (mille-feuille) / **66-67:** Mila Atkovska/Shutterstock (escargots); theendup/Shutterstock (restaurant) / **68:** violleta/Getty Images / **69:** bhofack2/Getty Images (bánh mi); Franck Legros/Getty Images (tagine) / **70-71:** Kiev.Victor/Shutterstock / **72:** HJBC/Shutterstock (Guerlain); Benny Marty/Shutterstock (people shopping) / **73:** Resul Muslu/Shutterstock (macarons); Romain P19/Shutterstock (Fouquet's) / **74-75:** Oliver Foerstner/Shutterstock (cyclists); Migel/Shutterstock (cavalry at parade); Alexander J.E. Bradley/500px (fireworks) / **76-77:** Pigprox/Shutterstock / **78-79:** Gagandeep Ghuman/Getty Images (Petit Palais); Atlantide Phototravel/Getty Images (Grand Palais) / **80:** Pavliha/Getty Images / **81:** Daniel.Candal/Getty Images (obelisk); David Henry/Getty Images (fountain) / **82-83:** joe daniel price/Getty Images / **84-85:** Jimena Contreras/500px (Versailles exterior); Frederic Legrand - COMEO/Shutterstock (Hall of Mirrors) / **86:** s74/Shutterstock (Place des Vosges); Janet Steveley/Getty Images (Palais-Royal) / **87:** Image - Natasha Maiolo/Getty Images (Palais du Luxembourg); FreeProd33/Shutterstock (Palais de l'Élysée) / **88:** Maxal Tamor/Shutterstock / **89:** MARTIN Florent/Shutterstock (Panthéon); Alex_Mastro/Shutterstock (Montmartre Cemetery) / **90:** Olivier DJIANN/Getty Images / **91:** MDoculus/Getty Images (street); mikroman6/Getty Images (illustration) / **92-93:** EQRoy/Shutterstock (Musée Marmottan Monet); Sailorr/Shutterstock (Centre Pompidou) / **94-95:** Julien Fourniol/Baloulumix/Getty Images / **96-97:** Maxime Mercier/Getty Images (manatee); Rrrainbow/Getty Images (Jardin des Plantes) / **98:** Tommy Larey/Shutterstock / **99:** Photo 12/Alamy Stock Photo (Aquaboulevard); Pawel Libera/Getty Images (Paris Plages) / **100-101:** Nattee Chalermtiragool/Shutterstock (Sacré-Coeur); MaxOzerov/Getty Images (Moulin Rouge) / **102-103:** by Mark Spowart/Getty Images (jellies); Rrrainbow/Shutterstock (dinosaurs); CoreyFord/Getty Images (*Compsognathus*) / **104:** River Thompson/Lonely Planet (café); Artem Avetisyan/Shutterstock (Latin Quarter) / **105:** OlegAlbinsky/Getty Images (café); Paul Maguire/Shutterstock (shopping) / **106-107:** Bruno De Hogues/Getty Images / **108:** Matt Mason/Getty Images (kestrel); jptinoco/Getty Images (Promenade Plantée) / **109:** River Thompson/Lonely Planet (Petite Ceinture); Matt Munro/Lonely Planet (Parc des Buttes-Chaumont) / **110-111:** Kiev.Victor/Shutterstock (Jardin des Serres d'Auteuil); EschCollection/Getty Images (Jardin des Tuileries) / **112-113:** MasterLu/Getty Images / **114:** Hung Chung Chih/Shutterstock / **115:** OlegAlbinsky/Getty Images (fountain); Alina Zamogilnykh/Shutterstock (mosaic) / **116:** UlyssePixel/Shutterstock / **117:** photofort 77/Shutterstock (Île de Loisirs de Bois-le-Roi); JOEL SAGET/AFP/Getty Images (sailboats) /

118-119: Jean-Francois Dumas/500px / **120-121:** bhcvn/Shutterstock (rat); By Skreidzeleu/Shutterstock (catacombs) / **122-123:** gabriel12/Shutterstock (market); Marco_Piunti/Getty Images (Futuro House) / **124-125:** Karl F Schofmann/Imagebroker/Shutterstock (Deyrolle); steve estvanik/Shutterstock (tapestry) / **126:** Elena Dijour/Getty Images (bookstore); Eric Schaeffer/Getty Images (mosque) / **127:** peterkirillov/Getty Images (statue); Cesarz/Shutterstock (frog legs) / **128:** Delpixart/Getty Images / **129:** Chesnot/Getty Images (heart); Anamaria Mejia/Shutterstock (wall) / **130-131:** olrat/Shutterstock / **132-133:** maziarz/Shutterstock / **141:** Tomas Marek/Shutterstock

WHAT'S THE DIFFERENCE? ANSWERS

140 A Kid's Guide to PARIS

IMAGE: A boat on the Seine by Notre-Dame Cathedral.

According to ancient Gallic mythology, the goddess of the Seine is named Sequana.